Haril

Tattva-viveka

Śrī Sac-cid-ānandānubhūti

Awakened Intelligence in AbsoluteTruth

Realization of the Eternally Existing, Fully Enlightened, Blissful Supreme

by Śrīla Bhaktivinoda Ṭhākura

THE VAISHNAVA FOUNDATION
United States/Slovenia/Australia

The Metamorphosis League for Monastic Studies:

The Vaishnava Foundation, Inc.

The Vaishnava Foundation presents

Tattva-viveka: Awakened Intelligence in Absolute Truth

Produced by Vaishnava Press Publications

Second Edition 2012

Limited printing

ISBN 978-1463733513

Contacts for the Vaishnava Foundation:

Snail Mail: 1360 W. Main St., Galesburg, IL 61401-3316

Email in United States:	vaishnava@therealexplanation.org
Email in Slovenia:	vaishnava@therealexplanation.org
Email in India:	rajk91@gmail.com
Email in Australia:	noldoli@gmail.com
English Websites:	therealexplantion.org
	returntosquareone.com
Slovenian Website:	zavestkrisne.tk
Croatian Website:	zavestkrisne.tk/hrvatski
Gujarati Website:	http://therealexplanation.org/krishnachetna

Dedication

To His Divine Grace A. C. Bhaktivedānta Swami Prabhupāda, without whose divine blessings, service, and mercy we would not have been able to come into contact with the potent spiritual teachings of Śrīla Bhaktivinode Ṭhākur.

oṁ ajñāna-timirāndhasya jñānāñjana śalākayā
cakṣur unmīlitaṁ yena tasmai śrī gurave namaḥ

Table of contents

Preface 7
Chapter One 9
Chapter Two..63
Appendix One 83
Appendix Two 90
Appendix Three..94
Appendix Four..108

Acknowledgments

To Bhakta Ernest Dras for propagating its teachings and this book on the Vaishnava Foundation website that he manages and for the diligent, expert, and time-consuming efforts he has put into the manuscript, together with his arranging its printing and covering all associated costs, and to Bhakta Joseph Crowl for his enthusiastic support of this project and procurement of an important subsidiary manuscript.

Please chant:

Hare Kṛṣṇa Hare Kṛṣṇa
Kṛṣṇa Kṛṣṇa Hare Hare
Hare Rāma Hare Rāma
Rāma Rāma Hare Hare

and be happy!

Vaikuṇṭheti para-vaikuṇṭheti goloketi śabdyate

Preface

Śrī Śrī Guru-Gaurāṅga jayataḥ

It is with great fortune and transcendental pleasure that we now present this English rendition of Tattva-viveka, a concise masterpiece revealed by His Divine Grace Śrīla Bhaktivinode Ṭhākur in 1893. The book consists of two chapters, called as ***Realization of Eternity*** and ***Realization of Eternal Consciousness***. Chapter One contains thirty-three Sanskrit verses, and Chapter Two contains fifteen. Of the total forty-eight, thirty-eight verses contain purports or commentaries, some of which are quite extensive. The original commentaries were in Bengali.

The treatise seeks to awaken higher intelligence within its reader. Human beings can be divided in many ways, and one such division is those who are actually awakened to spiritual reality (udita-viveka) and those who are still asleep to it (anudita-viveka). The Supreme Personality of Godhead, Lord Śrī Kṛṣṇa, in Bhagavad-gītā, describes the fully-realized and devoted sage as one who is sthita-prajña. His higher intelligence is fixed in the Absolute Truth at all times and in all circumstances. To have viveka awakened is a stage previous to sthita-prajña, but it is, nonetheless, both an important and essential development.

The Ṭhākur was a fully devoted representative of the most recent incarnation of the Supreme Lord, Śrī Caitanya Mahāprabhu, and he glorifies Him in the opening verses of each chapter. This edition also contains unique addenda in the form of four appendices, which cover topics directly relevant to the subject matter discussed. Appendix Four is a biographical sketch of the author's life and precepts. Two previous translations of this important work were consulted in order to perfect this particular edition.

Tattva-viveka is a special dispensation for the intellectual seeker of the Absolute, be he merely inquisitive or actually already learned to some extent. It meets a need for satisfying the spiritual hunger of a keen intelligence, one that will not accept anything less than a comprehensive and correct understanding of who we are, why we are forced to suffer, what is this universe, and what is our relationship with material nature. The book is surprisingly thorough and concise at the same time; indeed, it can be read cover-to-cover in one sitting.

It was designed by the Ṭhākur to not only answer the abovementioned inquiries concerning the meaning of life but was also tailored to transform an intelligent, good, and diligent man into a devoted sage, eligible to realize the Absolute Truth in this lifetime. If our translations and appendices help to realize that goal of Śrīla Bhaktivinode—for even one Westerner—then we shall consider this attempt successful in every way, shape, and form.

OM TAT SAT

Kailāsa Candra dāsa
Vaiṣṇava Foundation, editor
Completed July 14, 2011 on Guru-Pūrṇimā

Chapter One

Prathamānubhava: First Realization

Realization of Eternity

jayati sac-cid-ānanda-rasānubhava-vigrahaḥ /
procyate sac-cid-ānandānubhūtir yat-prasādataḥ //1//

All glories to Lord Śrī Caitanya Mahāprabhu, the nectarean form of everlasting knowledge and spiritual pleasure, by Whose mercy this realization of the eternally existing, fully enlightened, blissful Supreme has been transcribed.

ko 'haṁ vā kiṁ idaṁ viśvam āvayoh ko 'nvayo dhruvam /
ātmānaṁ nivṛto jīvaḥ pṛcchati jñāna-siddhaye //2//

"What is this universe or who am I? What fixed relationship is there between the us?" In order to find the Truth, the conditioned spirit soul, surrounded by matter, asks himself (these questions).

Purport

The external world of sense objects is perceived by the senses; these objects are called viṣaya, and, as a child matures, he becomes more and more aware of them. He becomes attracted to them, because he tastes pleasure in contact with them. As such, he thinks and acts continuously so he can experience this pleasure; he acts for nothing else. He becomes a constant companion of smell, taste, form, touch, and sound, and his mind thus becomes enslaved by them.

Then an idea arises: "When death comes, I will no longer have any relationship with these external sense objects." When this thought manifests, if he is fortunate, he turns away from the external world of sense objects and strongly desires to know the Absolute Truth. At that time, he asks the abovementioned three questions: "Who am I, the perceiver of this external world? What is this external world, and just what is my relationship to it?"

ātmā prakṛti-vaicitryād dadāti citram uttaram /
sva-svarūpa-sthito hy ātmā dadāti yuktam uttaram //3//

The self, due to the variegated nature of his conditioning, gives many, many answers (to these questions). The spirit soul situated in his own original form and nature indeed presents the true answer.

Purport

Both scripture and philosophy attempt to answer the three questions, and a fortunate person, who has turned away from sense objects, finds the answers to them. In India, these answers are delivered by Vedānta, the Vedas, and other literature which follows those scriptures.

Different answers, however, are provided by philosophies that misinterpret Vedic wisdom; examples of these are karma-mīmāṁsā, vaiśeṣika, nyāya, pātañjala, and pseudo-sāṅkhya.

Besides them, other answers to the questions are provided by philosophies that are in overt opposition to the Vedic wisdom, such as Buddhism and Cārvāka's atheistic philosophy. There are many philosophies giving many different answers, such as the answers of Materialism, Atheism, Pantheism, Secularism, Positivism, Skepticism, and Pessimism. These were promulgated in ancient China, Greece, Persia, as well as in France, Italy, England, Germany, and other countries throughout the world.

Logic was used by many philosophers to prove the existence of the Supreme. In other places, however, a concept was promulgated that one should simply believe in the Supreme Lord and worship Him. In many regions, a claim was made that its religion was originally delivered by the Supreme Lord. Some religions were anchored in the individual's own personal faith in the Supreme, and that is known as Theism. Christianity and Islam are among the religions with scriptures and belief systems given by the Supreme.

Answers to the three questions are actually of two different types: The answer given by the liberated spirit soul, situated in his original form and nature, and the great variety of differing answers given by all those who are or were not situated like this. Why not one single answer? The reason is that true answers are only given by a purified personality, one who is situated in his original, spiritual form and nature. All persons so situated will give the same answers, but fallen souls are not situated in their original spiritual forms and natures. The material realm is not their actual home.

The para-tattva or Supreme Truth has a parā-śakti, a higher, spiritual potency. Māyā-śakti, the potency of illusion, is the shadow potency of that parā-śakti and is the mother of the external world. Fallen spirit souls residing in this external world accept a great variety of material qualities offered by māyā-śakti, and they believe these qualities as their own. They accept a specific mixture of these qualities and an identity offered by māyā-śakti. In this way, the conditioned soul identifies with matter and his original qualities are withdrawn.

Material ideas are mixed with spiritual ideas in the mind of the conditioned soul in different ways. As such, the conditioned souls, misidentifying with a different mixture of material qualities, give their own answers to the abovementioned questions.

Thus are manifest a great variety of different answers, influenced by association, language, cultural activities, tradition, foods, and various patterns of thought in the countries where the conditioned souls reside. Time, place, and circumstance in this way amalgamate to form many variegated natures.

At the very beginning, spirit souls come into contact with matter in different ways. These different contacts bring about one set of variegatedness in nature. Next, another set of variations transpires due to differing countries, families, languages, and other related circumstances; the original variety of natures thus becomes multiplied by further variety. Only the person who has traveled to and learned all of these languages, and who has studied the history of each of those countries, could actually understand the scope of this multiplicity. I shall only direct your attention to that variety; it would be very troublesome to do more than this.

In relation to the abovementioned two kinds of answers, only one of them is the true answer. The other is according to many different philosophies and thus contains a great variety of answers. That extensive variegatedness may also be divided into two: The first group is called jñāna, and the other group, karma.

Someone may then protest: "You imply that you honor yukti or logic as the way to know Truth. Logic begits the other great variety of answers. Why then don't you also accept them?"

I respond to this protest as follows: Spiritual logic does not depend upon material logic, which begits a great variety of answers. As such, when I use the terms yukti and yukta, logic and Truth, I am referring to that logic and Truth accepted by liberated souls who are completely pure and no longer affected by the touch of material nature. That logic and Truth distinguishes precisely between matter and spirit. Taking shelter of matter, material logic inevitably leads to a great variety of conclusions. The genuine, true answer, the actually logical answer, is delivered by a liberated spirit soul situated in his original spiritual form and nature.

The other group, known as jñāna, is seen amongst the great variety of answers. The conditioned soul tries to distinguish between spirit and matter by utilizing jñāna. When that jñāna articulates positively, it is anvaya. It asserts that matter is the root of everything, primal, and beginningless. When that jñāna articulates negatively, it is vyatireka. It says that matter is simply a transformation of brahman, which has no potencies, and that matter cannot be annihilated. The followers of the other group of answers, known as karma, assert that souls here should engage themselves in material activities, because a Supreme Person does not exist.

The pure form of jñāna and karma have their place in genuine spiritual love and action. They are both part of the true answers to the abovementioned three questions. These pure forms will be discussed subsequently in our work. Words are unable to completely describe the pure Absolute Truth, because they are material in nature.

citraṁ bahu-vidhaṁ viddhi yuktam ekaṁ svarūpataḥ /
citram ādau tathā cānte yuktam eva vivicyate //4//

Know that the great variety (of answers) are many, and the Truth is fundamentally one. (In this work) first is considered the great variety (of answers) and then, at the end, certainly the right answer is considered.

ātmāthavā jaḍaṁ sarvaṁ svabhāvād dhi pravartate /
svabhāvo vidyate nityaṁ īśa-jñānaṁ nirarthakam //5//

(Some say) all is matter or the soul's own nature is naturally manifest as matter. Eternal knowledge of the Supreme is meaningless.

sarvathā ceśvarāsiddhir īśa-kartā prayojanāt /
para-loka-kathā mithyā dhūrtānāṁ kalpaneritā //6//

(They say) the required proof of a Supreme Controller and Creator is lacking in all respects. Talk of a spiritual world is false, reverberated according to the imagination of rascals.

samyogāj jaḍa-tattvānāṁ ātmā caitanya-saṁjñitaḥ /
pradurbhavati dharmo 'yaṁ nihito jaḍa-vastuni //7//

The self, evidenced as consciousness, is manifested from the elements of matter. His integral function is situated in matter.

viyogāt sa punas tatra gacchaty eva na saṁśayaḥ /
na tasya punar āvṛttir na muktir jñāna-lakṣaṇā //8//

At death, that (consciousness), without a doubt, again certainly merges into matter. He does not return, nor is there any liberation for the man possessing transcendental knowledge.

Purport

Materialism is widespread amongst the great variety of philosophies, and it can also be divided into two: 1) jadānanda-vāda or the philosophy of enjoyment, and 2) jada-nirvāṇa-vāda or the philosophy of complete cessation of material existence. At this time, we shall consider these two materialistic philosophies.

In the beginning and in a generic way, let us look at Materialism. It asserts that both consciousness and matter exist, but that consciousness is created from matter and did not exist before matter. All materialistic philosophies assert this. Inert matter is proclaimed to be eternal according to Materialism, and philosophies dealing with a Supreme Lord uselessly waste valuable time. Talk about a Supreme Lord only exists in that individual's imagination, because, if there is some supposedly supreme "Controller," then one is obliged to keep searching for a higher "Controller" who controls that "Controller."

The existence of a Supreme Lord has never been proved, and religious books throughout the world describing the Supreme and the spirit soul's residence in an eternal world are nothing more than a display of wild imagination by various and assorted rascals. Whatever they describe has no actual existence.

As such, Materialism also asserts that words like ātmā and caitanya, self and consciousness, only refer to matter in its particular aspects. These terms are created by a variegated pattern of forward or backward interactions of dead elements, known as anuloma and viloma, respectively. When anuloma in nature, self and consciousness are created. When viloma in nature, both of these are then merged back into matter, and, due to this, reincarnation is not at all possible.

Learning about the Absolute Truth or brahman cannot make liberation possible either, because the self is the same as matter and cannot be liberated from it. Ultimate reality is inert matter, and everything that exists is only a different aspect of it, part of its variegated nature.

These are the ideas accepted by all atheists.

One group of them advocates that individual material pleasure must be a man's goal in life. The other group, which realizes the pathetic futility and temporariness of such pleasure, searches for happiness in the cessation of existence, nirvāṇa. First, let us consider jadānanda-vāda, the philosophy of material pleasure. It is also of two kinds: 1) Selfish pleasure or svārtha-jaḍānanda-vāda, and 2) Unselfish pleasure or niḥsvārtha-jaḍānanda-vāda.

Those who adhere to the path of svārtha-jaḍānanda-vāda think in this way: "A Supreme Lord does not exist nor does any life after death, nor any ātmā, nor any reactions to activities. As such, since the only thing to be concerned about are results attained here in this world, let us spend our time in sense pleasures. There is no need to waste our time in the execution of ineffective religious activities." Due to bad association and sinful reactions, such atheistic thinking has existed in human society since antiquity. Faithful and respectable people have never allowed this philosophy to become prominent in their lives, however. Nevertheless, people in different countries have attempted to take shelter of this concoction; they have even written books promulgating it.

We find atheistic ideas promulgated in India by a brahmin named Cārvāka, in China by an atheist named Yangchoo, in Greece by the atheist Leucippus. In the central part of Asia, Sardanapolus propounded atheism, as did Lucretius in Rome. All of these men wrotes books propounding atheistic ideas, as did many other people in other countries. By acting to make others happy, Von Holbach says that a person should execute philanthropic deeds. This increases one's own happiness, which he considers a good thing. Atheistic authors of modern books promulgating svārtha-jaḍānanda-vāda, writing about unselfish pleasure or acting materially for securing good things for others, attempt to persuade people in general to believe in it.

Atheism has existed in India since antiquity. One philosopher, in a very erudite way, wrote a great distortion of the Vedic teaching, known as the <u>Mīmāṁsā-sūtras</u>. It begins with codanā-lakṣaṇo dharmaḥ, words that replace the Supreme with some kind of "abstract origin, nothing before this existing." It is called apūrva.

Democritus, a Greek philosopher, promulgated it in Greece, as well. He claimed that there was matter, there was the void, and that both exist eternally. He went on to say that, when matter and void meet, there is creation; when they are separated, then creation is destroyed. He said that the material elements are differentiated due to the different sizes of the atoms comprising those elements. Except for this, the elements are not actually different. He said that knowledge is a sensation; it comes into existence when something that is within touches that which is without. The philosophy of Democritus maintains that atoms compose all of existence.

In our country of India, there is the vaiśeṣika philosophy taught by Kaṇāda. He also said that eternal atoms compose material elements. Nevertheless, the atomic theory of Democritus and the vaiśeṣika philosophy of Kaṇāda are different. The vaiśeṣika philosophy maintains that there is an eternal existence of a soul.

In Greece, however, both Plato and Aristotle refused to accept a Supreme Eternal Controller as the sole creator of the material world. Their views can be seen in Kaṇāda's errors, also. Gassendi accepted that atoms exist, but he concluded that the Supreme Lord created them.

In France, both Diderot and La Mettrie pushed a theory of unselfish material pleasure. The niḥsvārtha-jaḍānanda-vāda idea reached its apex with Comte, a French philosopher born in 1795. He died in 1857. His contaminated philosophy is called Positivism; it is inappropriately named. It accepts only the existence of matter. It further claims that there is no true knowledge except for knowledge attained by the senses. It says that the mind only consists of material elements in a special arrangement. In the end, Comte concludes that the origin of existence cannot be described.

He goes on to say that there is no need to discover the origination of the material world. He claims that there is no indication or sign that a Conscious Being exists Who created the material world. He says that a discriminating mind should categorize everything according to their relationships, similarities, oppositions, and results, not accepting anything in existence beyond matter. Faith in a Supreme Lord is for children; adults know that the Supreme is a myth. Everyone should act righteously by discriminating between good and evil. The philosophy of material unselfish pleasure means that one should attempt to do good for all of humanity. That is the essence of niḥsvārtha-jaḍānanda-vāda.

With this frame of mind, Comte recommends that a person should imagine and worship the female form, even though, of course, it is unreal. Nevertheless, by such worship, good character is secured. The total earth is called the "Supreme Fetish." The land is known as the "Supreme Medium," and the original nature of a human being is called the "Supreme Being." Without seeking any selfish benefit, worshipping morning, noon, and night--in the past, present, and future—one should meditate upon this female form holding a baby, an imaginary form that is an amalgam of a person's mother, wife, and daughter.

The philosopher Mill of England[1] taught a similar sentimental philosophy like that of Comte's, a philosophy of material unselfish pleasure. Mill's atheistic Secularism attracted the minds of many English adolescents. Similar ideas were promulgated by not only Mill, but also by Lewis, Paine, Carlyle, Bentham, and Combe, along with other philosophers. These were of two kinds. The first was instructed by Holyoake, who, at least to some extent, benevolently accepted the existence of the Supreme. Bradlaugh, however, was a dyed-in-the-wool atheist who taught the other kind.

Although different in some ways, svārtha-jaḍānanda-vāda and niḥsvārtha-jaḍānanda-vāda are both materialistic. Materialism is seen to be both useless and indefensible when a person deeply ponders upon these speculations of the materialistic philosophers. Through the eyes of pure, spiritual logic, even glancing upon these ideas leads a person to reject them as indefensible and pathetic.

[1] Bhaktivinode is certainly referring to John Stuart Mill here, and not Mill's father or wife, both of whom were also somewhat well-known philosophers during his day. For more on Mill, c.f., Appendix Three.

Even logic that is merely ordinary will expose these notions as indefensible. They must be repudiated, and this is observed in the following ways:

1) Materialism searches for the root of everything as a unified principle, but this a cumbersome, frivolous undertaking. If one considers material atoms and the void eternal, the relationship between them is unable to be conceived. If one considers the power, quality, and action of material atoms to be eternal—without beginning and forever existing—then he cannot consider that the material world was ever even created. Any person who embraces these ideas is unable to consolidate the material world into an indivisible, underlying principle.

As such, he must believe that many simultaneous principles underlie the material world. He is without the power to know or elucidate what time is. His effort to locate an indivisible, underlying principle that controls the material world is merely the reckless prattle of a child.

2) Materialism is neither natural nor scientific. It is not intrinsic to nature, because everything in nature has a cause. It is most illogical to assume that matter is eternal and the cause of consciousness, that consciousness is merely a by-product of matter. The manifestation of causes and their effects is intrinsic to the world of gross matter. Materialism is unscientific, because consciousness manipulates and controls matter, which is jada or inert. Therefore, the conception that consciousness is only a by-product of this inert matter is violently in opposition to the principle of real scientific thought.

3) Consciousness is intrinsically superior to dead matter; only fools espouse it as a by-product of matter. Professor Ferris has lucidly explained all of this.

4) Can any person prove that inert matter is eternal? One Professor Tyndall has said that there is evidence to prove it. However, if anybody claims that he has seen forever into the past and into the future—and therefore has realized that inert matter is eternal—nobody should believe him.

5) Both Molescott and Buchner assert that inert matter is eternal, but their claim is nothing more than an imagination inside their craniums. When in time matter no longer exists, their speculations will be transformed into lies.

6) Comte writes: "We should make no attempt to discover either matter's origin or destination; such an effort is nothing more than adolescent curiosity." Since a living being is naturally conscious, however, he is, by his very nature, curious about these very things. He cannot conduct a funeral ceremony to exalt the death of his own curiosity. The mother of real knowledge entails a search for causes and their effects. If Comte's assertion is endorsed, human intelligence will be eradicated within but a few days; there can be no doubt about this. At that time, humans will have devolved into stunted, stupefied beings without the power to think.

7) Nobody has ever witnessed human consciousness generated from inert material elements; only idiots believe this will happen sometime in the future. In the manuscript I am holding in my hand, a book of history that details the previous three-thousand years, no one during that time has reported ever witnessing human life generating spontaneously from the interactions of material elements. If human consciousness is created spontaneously from dull matter, at least someone should have spontaneously manifested from material nature during all of those years.

8) The elegant and congruous arrangement of humans, animals, trees, and all the other life forms of this material world indicates a Supreme Creator and Controller. Seeing this, there must be a Supreme Creator, Who is also Supremely Conscious.

The philosophy of Materialism is disproved even by ordinary logic; only very unlucky individuals accept it. They have no concept of spiritual happiness, and their material desires are quite small and contemptible. The philosophy of material cessation will be described subsequently in our work.

kartavyo laukiko dharmaḥ pāpānāṁ viratir yataḥ /
vidvadbhir lakṣito nityo svabhāva-vihito vidhiḥ //9//

(Materialists opine that) ethics and morality should be followed, because they bring about the cessation of sins. The wise see that eternal rules of morality are already situated within human nature.

puṅkhānupuṅkhā-rūpeṇa jijñāsyo sa sukhāptaye /
jīvane yat sukhaṁ tat tu jīvanasya prayojanam //10//

(Materialists similarly say) through painstaking effort, the attainment of material happiness should be inquired into. In this lifetime, that happiness is indeed the goal of living.

jīvane yat kṛtaṁ karma jīvanānte tad eva hi /
jagatām anya-jīvānāṁ sambandhe phala-daṁ bhāvet //11//

At the end of life, the activities he has executed will indeed deliver a fruitful result for all others who had a relationship with him.

na karma nāśam āyāti yadā vā yena vā kṛtam /
apūrva-śakti-rūpeṇa kurute sarvam unnatam //12//

Whenever or by whoever performed, no action is destroyed. By the form of an abstract power within them, they cause all to be elevated.

Purport

We shall now ponder upon the ordinary activities of those who are adherents of the philosophy of Materialism. They claim: "Even though there is no Supreme Lord, no self, and no existence after this spot life, humans should still adhere to moral and ethical rules. By acting in that way, one will be happy in this life; by not acting morally or ethically, one will find himself in a fearful circumstance. Immoral activities are also known as sins. A person who unselfishly acts to make others happy will find that his own happiness automatically follows such unselfish action."

The conclusion is that a person should follow the principles of morality and ethics, casting sins to a distance, for they bring only harassment and miseries. Material nature has its own set of laws. Therefore, everyone should follow those laws, since everyone is a part of nature. All philosophers should attempt to uncover laws governing the material realm. The highest happiness here is the result of pious deeds done to attain that happiness. To attain this happiness for oneself, a person should, with painstaking effort, attempt to uncover and then adhere to the laws of material nature.

If you cavil: 'But I'll not exist after death, so why should I, renouncing my own unrestricted pleasure, adhere to the rules of ethics and morality?' Then I reply: 'Your actions are not futile; even after your demise, they will not cease delivering results to other people. After your death, they will bring a variety of results to different people in this world. If you married and produced children, giving them an education which instructed them in ethics and morality, then those actions will deliver results enjoyed by many. If, after earning money, you construct hostels, schools, roads, spas, and other similar amenities, then these results of your actions will be enjoyed by many people.'

If you object: 'The results of those actions will swiftly terminate,' then I reply: 'Why not act? Your actions are interminable. When matured, actions have a very marvelous power that will make this never-ending world a most outstanding place. As such, you must act without selfish motivations.'"

Materialism craters of its own accord, just like a structure without walls or foundation. Nobody will adhere to a religious system without hope of, or fear for, what will happen at the end of life. As its very name demonstrates, the adherents of svārtha-jadānanda-vāda, the philosophy of selfish material pleasures, are all themselves selfish. Indeed, the adherents of niḥsvārtha-jadānanda-vāda, the philosophy of unselfish material pleasures, are, in fact, selfish as well. It is impossible to adhere to the concept of unselfish material pleasures for very long.

The philosopher Von Holbach composed System of Nature in 1770 under the nom d'guerre Mirabond. In that book, he wrote: "In this world, unselfishness does not exist. I say in good faith that one becomes happy by means of the happiness of others." I also see it that way. There is no meaning to the idea of unselfish Materialism; it is like a flower imagined to be floating in the sky. Unselfishness is utilized only to attain one's own personal happiness, as well as freedom from distresses. Such a person thinks: "People will trust me if they hear I am unselfish, and then I shall readily attain my goals." A mother or brother's love, friendship, or the love between man and woman—are any of these actually unselfish? These examples of "love" do not last if they do not bring about one's own personal happiness.

To attain eternal bliss at the end, some pass all of their lives in tyāga or renunciation, but every religious or philosophical system is based upon selfishness. Love for the Supreme Person is also selfish. It is everybody's nature to be selfish. The phrase "one's own nature" indicates selfishness. Selfishness is intrinsic to one's state of being; unselfishness is unnatural. As such, it is truly never witnessed.

Nobody would engage in action without hope for a future happiness in a future life. Those of purified intelligence have no attraction to the apūrva philosophy of Jaimini or any life-force idea of Western speculators. Anyone who adheres to these is eventually cheated.

Even the smārta-paṇḍits of India, who quote Jaimini's philosophy of apūrva in their writings, themselves all believe in the grace of the Supreme, as well as in a life of bliss in the spiritual world. They would all turn their backs immediately on Jaimini if they knew that Jaimini's philosophy of apūrva is opposed even to the existence of a Supreme Lord. Jaimini realized profoundly that belief in the Supreme remains in the hearts of humanity. As such, he shrewdly and carefully created an imaginary "God" in his apūrva philosophy, one who grants the results of actions. Therefore, hidden under the veil of belief in this Supreme, the atheistic karma-mīmāṁsā philosophy pushed by the smārta-paṇḍitas has a powerful following in India.

Somebody's self-interest often clashes with somebody else's self-interest. A person of mean intelligence becomes attracted upon hearing the term "unselfishness," because he speculates that, by following this philosophy, his own desires will be fulfilled. That is another rationale as to why the philosophy of atheistic Materialism has become widespread. It is not easily understood how the preacher of unselfish material pleasure induces his devotees to act ethically and morally in this world. Impelled by their own selfish desires, such people may act ethically and morally for some limited time, but, when they deliberate on it, they will eventually engage in sin.

They will say to themselves: "Don't refrain from sensual pleasure, O Brother. Enjoy them as you like, as long as others do not find out about that. Why not? I do not believe the world will self-destruct because of them. There is no Omniscient, Supreme Lord giving us the results of our activities. What do you have to fear? Just be a bit cautious, so that no one will find out. If they learn about it, then you will forfeit your good reputation. Perhaps evil men or the government will then put you in distress. Neither you nor others will be happy if that transpires."

Know it certainly that, if the hearts of those pushing atheistic ethics and morality were examined, these deliberations would be found in them. For example, one day a smārta-paṇḍita prescribed the candrāyana vow, along with other harsh penances, to an inquirer who asked him the process for forgiveness of a specific sin. Hearing this remedy, the inquirer replied: "Mahāśaya Bhaṭṭācārya, if I must perform the candrāyana vow for terminating the life of that spider, then your own son, who was implicated in the act, must also perform it."

Realizing that this would be a disaster for his son, the Bhaṭṭācārya turned two or four pages in his big book and exclaimed: "Aha, I made a mistake! Now I see here that the book says a dead spider is nothing more than piece of rag. As such, you have no need to perform any atonement whatsoever!" Atheistic smārta-paṇḍitas are just like that.

They sometimes accept an afterlife and worship of the Lord, Who gives the results of all action, but they believe that these two ideas are only subordinate parts to their atheist philosophy.

Bhakti or pure devotional service is never found in their concepts. Instead, it is seen that, what in the beginning was unselfishness, is gradually transformed into selfishness. To prevent this, some atheistic karma-mīmāṁsā speculators accept the existence of one omniscient Supreme Controller, Who bestows the results of activities. They go on to quote many scriptural passages in order to demonstrate that worship of this Supreme is a part of the philosophy of karma-mīmāṁsā.

They accept an imaginary Supreme Lord in this way. Afraid that his ethics and morality would not be taken seriously, Comte conjured up a so-called "God" that would be considered real. Comte was more honest; Jaimini more farsighted. Comte's conjure was spotted, and, as such, his concept of imaginary God worship never attracted much of a following. Jaimini had a more profound understanding of the situation. Therefore, karma-mīmāṁsā gained wide acceptance amongst the smārta-paṇḍitas. When all is said and done, both Comte and Jaimini adhered to the same philosophy.

If a person scrutinizes the concepts and actions of the smārta-paṇḍitas, he will see that karma-mīmāṁsā is indefensible. Why is that so? It is indefensible, because it can never bring real auspiciousness to humanity. Neither Secularism, Positivism, nor karma-mīmāṁsā have the power to uproot sins. Again and again, karma-mīmāṁsā spouts devotion to the Supreme, such as: "I am Your follower, and I make it so that other people can become qualified to follow You. I purify the sinners, placing them at Your feet." These are only cheating statements.

They are not at all sincere. Real pious activity or true karma is devotional service or bhakti to the Supreme. As long as activity keeps calling itself "karma," it is not part of bhakti. When it actually is part of devotional service, karma then calls itself bhakti. As long as it continues to call itself "karma," it is a rival of bhakti, always trying to make itself more important than bhakti. Karma propounds that it assists civilization, art, and philosophy. When karma actually transforms into bhakti, it then makes philosophy, art, and civilization more grand and majestic. I shall not discuss this in any more detail here.

bhavaḥ kleśo 'bhavaḥ keṣāṁ mate saukhyam iti sthitam /
nirvāṇa-sukha-samprāptiḥ śarīra-kleśa-sādhanāt //13//

Material existence is suffering. Some think becoming situated in non-existence is happiness. Due to the activities of the body bringing misery, (they believe) happiness is attained in cessation of existence.

Purport

Some think existence as suffering and happiness coming when material existence ceases. Due to the body bringing so much suffering, they think that they can become happy by such cessation. Materialists will search for material pleasures as long as they find pleasure in material things. They will thus seek the drab pleasures of the material realm, whether selfish or supposedly unselfish. In truth, however, material pleasures are meaningless and pathetic, incompatible to spiritual substance.

Amongst these materialists, those who are actually intelligent are unable to find any satisfaction in material pleasures. However, ignorant of spiritual existence, how is it possible for them to search for never-ending spiritual pleasures? As such, they consider that nirvāṇa, or material cessation, is the sole happiness and to that they run. They opine: "Material existence is suffering, and cessation of existence is happiness. Due to this material body bringing only misery, let us endeavor for the happiness of nirvāṇa, material cessation."

When atheistic karma-mīmāṁsā, seeking material pleasure, was very prominent in India, the Vedas, brimming with spiritual truths, were believed to be the only true scriptures. At that time, under the claim that the Vedas promulgated atheistic karma-mīmāṁsā, many materialistic brāhmins pursued sensual pleasures in this life—and society girls of Indra's heaven in the afterlife—by performing the sacrifices. It was then that a certain powerful personality named Śakyasiṁha, dissatisfied with material pleasures, was born into a warrior family. He decided one day that, since the sufferings of the material body cannot be escaped, real happiness rested only in nirvāṇa, material cessation. He founded jada-nirvāṇa-vāda, Buddhist philosophy.

That same philosophy of nirvāṇa was promulgated even before his time, and there is plenty of evidence to establish that fact. It was at his time, however, that the philosophy of Śakyasiṁha, the philosophy of material cessation, gathered many adherents. From that time onward, many promulgated and followed Buddhism. Nevertheless, Śakyasiṁha was not the only preacher of cessation of existence, because, either during or just a little before him, a personality named Jīna, born to a vaiśya or business family, preached something similar to Buddhism. His philosophy became known as Jainism, but it remained only in India.

Buddhism, however, crossed the oceans, rivers, and mountain ranges to enter China, Tatarsthan, Mynamar, Thailand, Ceylon, Japan, and many other lands. Even now, Buddhist philosophy is followed in many countries and has many branches. The ideas of the void, known as śūnya, and cessation of existence, known as nirvāṇa, are still heard and seen in all of these branches. Nevertheless, humans are unable to repudiate their intrinsic belief in the Supreme, so the Supreme Lord's worship is also observed in some of these Buddhist branches.

I once questioned a Buddhist monk from Mynamar, one who obviously did not assimilate the actual teachings of Buddhism. He answered my questions by replying: "The Supreme is without beginning, and He created this universe. He incarnated in the form of the Buddha into this world, and, again assuming His actual form as the Supreme, He returned to His heavenly abode. If we act with piety and follow the rules of our religion, then we shall also go there." From what this monk revealed to me, it was obvious that this Buddhist from Mynamar did not know the actual philosophy of his cult. In the name of the Buddhist philosophy, he only repeated common religious ideas that are intrinsic to the nature of all humanity.

Philosophy founded upon logical deceptions is unable to bring good to humanity. Such deceptive philosophy is cherished only in the hearts and writings of philosophical professionals. Ordinary people who claim to adhere to these philosophies will tend to revert back to common religious thoughts intrinsic to human nature. Comte's "universal love," Jaimini's karma-mīmāṁsā with its imaginary "God" of apūrva, and the jada-nirvāṇa-vāda of Śakyasiṁha, will all, in due course, be transformed by their adherents into religion that is common to that most intrinsic part of human nature. It is inevitable and taking place at this very time.

A philosophy similar to Buddhism and Jainism, called Pessimism, also a philosophy of material cessation, was promulgated in Europe as well. Know that Buddhism and Pessimism are not separate. In only one way are they actually different. Continuously suffering, the living being wanders in transmigration in Buddhist philosophy. By adhering to Buddhist principles, the conditioned soul gradually attains preliminary cessation of existence in nirvāṇa. Then, at the end, he attains complete cessation of existence in pari-nirvāṇa.

In Pessimism, however, the soul does not transmigrate. As such, the jada-nirvāṇa-vāda is twofold: 1) nirvāṇa after a single birth and death, and 2) nirvāṇa after many births and deaths.

Both Buddhism and Jainism obviously belong to the second group, because both accept transmigration. In Buddhism, after many births of practicing kindness and renouncing material things, the follower first becomes a bodhisattva and then, finally, a buddha. The soul eventually attains pari-nirvāṇa in jada-nirvāṇa-vāda by practicing meditation, humility, peace, tolerance, kindness, selflessness, friendliness, and renouncing material things. The soul no longer exists in pari-nirvāṇa, but in nirvāṇa the soul exists as a form of mercy.

The adherents of Jainism opine: "By practice of kindness and renouncing material things, by cultivating all the good virtues, the soul gradually moves through the stages of Nāradatva, Mahādevatva, Vāsudevatva, Paravāsudevatva, and Cakravartitva.

When the soul attains nirvāṇa at the end, he is Bhagavattva. Jainism and Buddhism both accept the following concepts:

1) The material world is eternal;
2) Karma is beginningless, but it can be brought to an end;
3) Existence is suffering;
4) Pari-nirvāṇa, or complete cessation of existence, is true happiness;
5) The karma-mīmāṁsā of Jaimini, under the mantle of Vedic authority, is inauspicious for all living beings;
6) Pari-nirvāṇa is auspicious for the all living beings, and
7) Indra and all the devas are servants of the wise seeking nirvāṇa, but they are masters over those who adhere to karma-mīmāṁsā.

Belonging to the first group of jada-nirvāṇa-vāda are both Schopenhauer and Hartmann. Schopenhauer's teaching was that, by abandoning the will to live and by fasting, becoming free from desires, renouncing material things, humility, physical mortification, and purity, the soul attains to nirvāṇa. Hartman claimed that there was no need for physical mortification, because, at the time of death, nirvāṇa is automatically attained. However, a philosopher called Benson preached that suffering is eternal and nirvāṇa impossible.

That brings us to the philosophy of Advaita, also known as Monism or Impersonalism. It is another kind of jada-nirvāṇa-vāda; it is also a materialistic philosophy. Every impersonalist hankers to end his personal existence and taste ānanda by merging into the impersonal brahman effulgence. That is their philosophy, but, after nirvāṇa, they would no longer exist. If they no longer exist, then they cannot experience anything--spiritual bliss or anything else.

Actually, Advaita philosophy is exactly like jada-nirvāṇa-vāda. The materialistic philosophy of cessation is completely indefensible, because it has not made a decision about the intrinsic nature of the individual soul. If such individuals are only creations of matter, the pitfall will be in accepting only the importance of material pleasures; that is cent-per-cent atheism. Conversely, if individuals are separate from matter and not dependent upon the transformations in it, then how can they ever cease to exist? Is there any evidence of this? Is there any evidence that persons who are not material—spirit souls—ever cease to exist?

When all is said and done, these philosophies are entirely atheistic. Those who preached so intensely this concept of nirvāṇa did so in order to terminate the wickedness of the karma-mīmāṁsā concoction. Due to the oppressive ways of the brāhmins with their embrace of the karma-mīmāṁsā concept, the warrior and other castes became very agitated, staging a philosophical revolt against the intellectual caste. That was the reason why all the warriors accepted Buddhism and all the mercantile class accepted Jainism.

When people separate into factions, hating one another accordingly, that hatred can indeed turn out to be extremely strong. Due to passionate factionalism, they no longer consider what is logical or what is illogical. That is the technique in which Buddhism and Jainism were propagated in India and other countries. Due to their being feeble in spiritual logic, they all believed that these nirvāṇa philosophies were sent to them by the Supreme. It is well-known in history that some of the European people who hated Christianity there also promulgated jada-nirvāṇa-vāda.

kecid vadanti māyā yā sā kartrī jagatāṁ kila/
cid-acit-savinī sūkṣmā śakti-rūpā sanātanī //14//

Some say that Māyā is what is indeed the creator of the universe, the mother of spirit and matter, the eternal, subtle form of power.

Purport

There are those who say: "Māyā, a potency without beginning or end, existing in a subtle form, created all the universes. She generated two principles: Spirit and matter." When the barren philosophy of Buddhism became prominent, this philosophy of Māyā was still able to endure, mutating into ever more novel forms. At the time, the tantra-śāstras gradually influenced Buddhism.

Then Māyāvāda was concocted, and, at that time, so-called Buddhism attached itself to the philosophy of the tantrics. Māyāvāda, which is actually covered Buddhism, was espoused amongst those who had not accepted Buddhism. The actions of the Māyāvādī-Vedāntists commenced when Māyāvāda, apparently based on the Vedas, was preached.

Māyāvāda was pushed in an entirely separate configuration in the mountainous region of India. It was spread in a form adhering to the Tantras, promulgated by its āchāryas as the philosophy of Māyā-śakti. Many opine that Tantra philosophy has emanated from pseudo-Kapila's philosophical presentation, but I do not agree with that. Although pseudo-Kapila consented that Prakṛti, material nature, is the creator of the universe, he also confirmed that spiritual truth is without beginning when he said of the Puruṣa ***puṣkara-palāśa-van nirlepaḥ***: "The Supreme is untouched by matter just as a lotus petal is untouched by water."

According to my perspective, Śaiva-siddhānta is what has evolved from pseudo-Kapila's Sāṅkhya philosophy. People with meager discriminatory power often make the mistake of thinking Śaiva-siddhānta and Tantra philosophy to be the same. In Śaiva-siddhānta, Prakṛti is particularly honored. The tantric munis conclude that Prakṛti is the mother who created spirit itself, despite the fact that, in Tantra philosophy, the Puruṣa and Prakṛti are compared to two halves of a chick-pea.

The tantric munis also have invented a kind of nirvāṇa where individual souls attain cessation of existence. Belief in the Supreme is not to be found in this philosophy that worships the material power. Those who worship the Supreme spiritual śakti offer prayers to the Omniscient Lord of All. The worshippers of material power, on the other hand, imitating and ridiculing those prayers, at times also offer prayers to Māyā. For example, Von Holbach, a dedicated atheist, offered these prayers to the Māyā-śakti:

"O Nature Personified, O Goddess of all the elements, O Form of Piety and Truth, who are Your two children, please become our protector always. May humanity sing of your glorious praises. O Goddess of Nature Personified, please place us on the path of Your pleasure and drive illusions far from our minds. Please cast evil from our hearts and prevent us from falling as we tread upon Your path of progress. Create for us a kingdom of real knowledge, deliver us goodness, and fix peace in our hearts." Von Holbach, a nature philosopher, also opines that neither a Supreme nor a soul nor an afterlife exists. He says that material nature or Māyā is the Parameśvarī, Supreme Regulatrix, and everybody should seek out his own personal happiness.

The Supreme Personality of Servitor Godhead, His Lordship Śiva, offers the following prayers to the original Māyā-śakti, the goddess Kālī, in the Mahā-nirvāṇa Tantra:

sṛṣṭer ādau tvam ekāsīt tamo-rūpam agocaram
tvatto jātaṁ jagat sarvaṁ para-brahma-sisṛkṣayā

"In the form of abject darkness, You alone existed at the beginning of the creation. By the desire of the Supreme Brahman, You created the entire universe."

The Mahā-nirvāna Tantra espouses the concept of Sāṅkhya, describing a Puruṣa aloof from matter but a Prakṛti active in the material world. In that Tantra, His Lordship Śiva informs Goddess Kālī:

punaḥ svarūpam āsādya tamo-rūpaṁ nirākṛtiḥ
vācātītaṁ mano-'gamyaṁ tvam ekaivāvaśiṣyate

"You manifest again in a form of darkness. You are beyond the power of mind or words to know or describe. When the worlds are no longer manifest and have dissolved, You become formless and are no longer manifest."

tvam eva jīvo loke 'smiṁs tvaṁ vidyā-para-devatā

"You are the individual conditioned souls here in this world. You are the Supreme Goddess of Knowledge Personified."

The individual conditioned souls are herein said to be non-different from Māyā, but this contradicts the siddhānta of Sāṅkhya philosophy:

yāvan na kṣiyate karma śubhaṁ vāśubham eva vā
tāvan na jāyate mokṣo nṛṇāṁ kalpa-śatair api

"As long as benefic and malefic karma is not annihilated, there can be no liberation for the conditioned souls, even after hundreds of millennia."

kurvāṇaḥ satataṁ karma kṛtvā kaṣṭa-śatāny api
tāvan na labhate mokṣaṁ yāvat jñānaṁ na vindati

"Even by performing hundreds of severe austerities and many pious acts over and over, if he has not achieved transcendental knowledge, the soul does not gain liberation."

jñānaṁ tattva-vicāreṇa niṣkāmenāpi karmaṇā
jāyate kṣīṇa-tapasāṁ viduṣāṁ nirmalātmanām

"By pious acts free from desire, wise and purified beings searching after Truth, fixed in austerity, attain transcendental knowledge."

na muktir japanād dhomād upavāsa-śatair api
brahmaivāham iti jñatvā mukto bhavati deha-bhṛt

"Even by japa, or the performance of sacrifices, or by hundreds of fasts, a person does not attain liberation. The embodied being becomes a liberated soul only by realizing, 'I am certainly brahman.'"

manasā kalpitā muktir nṛṇāṁ cen mokṣa-sādhanī
svalpa-labdhena rājyena rājāno mānavās tathā

"If, only by thinking themselves as being free, humans could attain liberation, then, by imagining that they have obtained a kingdom, they could all become kings as well."

jñānaṁ jñeyaṁ tathā jñātā tritayaṁ bhāti māyayā
vicāryamāṇe tritaye ātmaivaiko 'vaśiṣyate

"The three-fold aspects of knowledge, the object of knowledge, and the knower all issue forth from the power of illusion. Carefully discriminating amongst these three, understanding them properly, only the ātmā actually remains."

jñānam ātmaiva cid-rūpo jñeyam ātmaiva cin-mayaḥ
vijñātā svayam evātmā yo jānāti sa ātma-vit

"Know that the ātmā is knowledge, the ātmā is the object of knowledge, and the ātmā is the personal knower as well. A person who knows this is the knower of the ātmā."

The reality is that various Tantras espouse a great variety of philosophies. No one can say that every Tantra teaches worship of Māyā or Śakti-vāda; in some, that is accepted, in others, it is vehemently resisted. The Supreme Brahman is the Creator in some Tantras, whereas, in others, Prakṛti is the Creator. In others, the jīva or individual soul is the Creator. While some Tantras opine that individual souls are an illusion, others say that they are real.

It is said in some Tantras that the letter ṁ in the sacred syllable Oṁ is the Creator, in some others, that the Puruṣa and Prakṛti are both the Creators, while in other Tantras, Prakṛti is said to be the only Creator of everything.

Therefore, the conclusion must be that, because so many varying philosophies are espoused in the Tantras, none of them can be singled out as the sole tantric philosophy. In the abovementioned verse, we find the words ***sṛṣṭer ādau***: "It is said that, in the beginning of the creation before the material world was created, Prakṛti alone existed." Then it is stated that, by the desire of the Supreme Brahman, Prakṛiti created the material world. What is that Prakṛti? Who is that Supreme Brahman? Will the individual soul become that Supreme Brahman when he attains transcendental knowledge?

In the verse beginning with ***tvam eva jīvo loke 'smin***, it is claimed that the individual, conditioned souls are all identical with the material nature, but this makes no sense whatsoever. There is also described in the Tantras ritual illicit sex life, called latā-sādhana, ritual sex with consumption of meat, fish, and wine, called pañca-makāra-sādhana, and a ritual for imbibing wine known as surā-sādhana. What kind of religious rituals are these? I have no idea how can they be considered religious. These conceptions are similar to the atheism intrinsic to karma-mīmāṁsā or the imaginary goddess of material nature conjured by Comte. These kinds of Tantric worship are nothing more than the creation of someone's imagination. I shall say nothing more about it!

athavā bhāva eva syāt neśvaro na jagaj-janaḥ /
bhāvo nitya-vicitrātmā nābhāvo vidyate kvacit //15//

(Others say) "Ideas are indeed all there is--no Supreme Controller, no material world, nor any living entities. The self is an everlasting variety of ideas. Except for these ideas, nothing exists."

Purport

Some philosophers consider that only the ideas in their minds actually exist, and nothing else. They proclaim that the "objective world" apprehended by the senses does not actually exist. They declare that "subjective reality," or ideas, are what actually exist. They assert that no one should execute activities. Only ideas exist, and, in reality, nothing else. This philosophy of ideas was preached by Bishop Berkeley and other speculative philosophers; it is called Idealism. Mill accepted a modified version of it. It is completely inaccurate to claim that Idealism is the same as Spiritualism.

When someone thinks about information that has come from his senses, those thoughts are called ideas. Such ideas which arrive in this manner are nothing more than thoughts based upon contact of material senses with the material world; such thoughts are not connected to anything beyond that world. Collecting light that filters through the senses, the mind thinks and ideas emerge. As such, Idealism is not something superior to Materialism.

Amongst the Advaita-vādīs or impersonalists, some assert: "There is no Supreme, no world, nor any living entities. All of these things are ideas only, greatly variegated, without beginning or end. These ideas are eternal and Absolute Reality." This philosophy is both extremely pathetic and ridiculous—only a deranged person would have an inclination to believe it. If we scrutinize the lives of philosophers who propagate such opinions in their books, we shall see that, as far as their activities were concerned, they disbelieved the Idealism they promulgated. It is not inaccurate to state that ideas are matter in a subtle form. Therefore, Idealism must be grouped amongst the diverse varieties of Materialism.

satyam eva tv asan nityaṁ sad evānitya-bhāvanā /
kecid vadanti māyāndhāḥ yukti-vāda-parāyaṇāḥ //16//

Some, devoted to and blinded by the illusions of logic, say: "But what is true, in time becomes untrue; it is certainly always a temporary, relative truth."

Purport

Some philosophers expound on this perspective: "Whatever someone says to be 'true' is only temporarily so. As such, no truth is absolute or eternal; all truth is relative and temporary. What is thought to be true now will eventually be disproved and changed later. In the end, it will be regarded as an untruth. Therefore, the only changeless or absolute truth is the assertion that there is no absolute truth." This idea generates a guffaw of laughter, because there is no truth in it whatsoever. Blinded by illusions and addicted to the deceptions of logic, only some professional philosophers accept this ridiculous, illogical proposition.

These philosophers embrace the concept that Absolute Truth cannot exist, that truth is only relative. In Bengali, this concept is expressed by the slogan ***noyi hoy ebam hoyi noy***: "It is not this; it is not that." From this illogical idea, the philosophy of doubts emerges. In English, this is the philosophy of Skepticism preached by Hume and others. Although this philosophy of doubts or Skepticism is not at all natural and is indefensible, somehow or other, it has been accepted by many professional philosophers.

Jadānanda-vāda, the philosophy of material pleasure, and jada-nirvāṇa-vāda, the philosophy of cessation, had inflicted great evil upon their adherents. Therefore, people in general became overwhelmed with horror merely upon hearing their names. Intrinsic human nature is originally pure, wearing the decoration of bhakti or devotional service to the Supreme. In order to cleave its shackles, logic fabricated Scepticism, the philosophy of doubts.

By following Materialism, humans did not find joy. The philosophy of Materialism grabbed logic in this way, bound its hands and feet with solid shackles, and cast it into a gloomy prison cell. Materialism accepts that matter is eternal and all that exists. Professor Huxley preached the materialistic concept; since then, it has also issued forth from many other mouths.

These people assert: "No actual description of events can be promulgated without talking about material causes and effects. Without being based upon such causes and effects, neither can any conclusions be drawn. As such, in the end, words such as 'spirit' and 'love' will be cast far away from all literature. Then people will, in due course, be liberated in order to be carried off by the waves of Materialism. At that time, the very misconception of free will will be shackled and imprisoned, and the truth that all activities are determined by material laws will be proved beyond a shadow of a doubt."

When so many people started to speak illogically like this, human nature, realizing that it was about to descend into decadence, reversed itself and began to tread the path of a new and very different philosophy. "This new philosophy will bring us no negative results. Why? Because it will annihilate Materialism." Based upon this premise and promise, logic generated Scepticism, the philosophy of doubts. Skepticism cast the detritus of Materialism far away to a great distance.

However, Skepticism created another impediment to belief in the Supreme. It made people doubt as follows: "I have no power to see things as they actually are; I see only some aspects of these things. Where is the proof that I am seeing correctly? I perceive only limited aspects of things with my senses: With my eyes, form, with my ears, sound, with my nose, smell, with my skin, touch, and with my tongue, taste. I learn the quality of the things of this world through these five doors of sense knowledge, but, if I had more than these five—if I had, let's say, ten senses—I would perceive different things about the objects of the senses. In my current limited way, I have secured only some small portion of knowledge with my senses, but it is knowledge that is shot through with doubts."

In this way, even though Skepticism annihilated the philosophy of Materialism, it did not assist the cause of Real Transcendental Philosophy. Skepticism does not doubt that the material world exists. Instead, it only asserts: "I do not have comprehensive knowledge of the things of this world, and there is no possibility that I shall ever have such complete knowledge. The conclusion must be that I shall never understand things as they truly are."

In the end, Skepticism denies itself. If there is actual Truth to be understood, then what is the root from which this philosophy of doubts grows? With vigilant discrimination, one will realize that this philosophy of doubts is nothing more than idle, foolish talk.

"Do I exist or do not I exist?" Who is it that expresses the doubt? I am that person; therefore, I exist.

sarveṣāṁ nāstikānāṁ vai matam etat purātanam /
deśa-bhāṣā-vibhedena lakṣitaṁ ca pṛthak pṛthak //17//

From antiquity, within many different countries and many languages, many varieties of atheistic opinion have existed.

Purport

Three of the oldest systems of atheism are: 1) Materialism, the adoration of material nature, 2) Idealism, and 3) Skepticism. All other forms of atheism are included within these three. It is mistaken thinking to consider that modern systems of atheism are merely recent inventions. These same atheisms have existed since antiquity under different names and in different forms. Accordingly, a great variety of atheism was preached in our country, India. Of these, karma-mīmāṁsā, vaiśeṣika, and nyāya are overtly atheistic; Patañjali's philosophy of yoga and the Vedāntic monism of Advaita-vāda are covert or covered atheism. Since you may like to have a glimpse of these philosophies, we shall now concisely consider them.

Sāṅkhya: This very old philosophy was espoused by pseudo-Kapila in his book. Maharṣi Kapila says there:

Īśvarāsiddheḥ: "The Supreme's existence has not been perfectly proved." ***Kapila-sutra, 1.92.***

Mukta-baddhayor anyatarābhāvān na tat-siddhiḥ: "The Supreme is either conditioned or liberated, and nothing more than this can be said about it." ***Kapila-sutra, 1.93.***

The Supreme Lord is either liberated or conditioned? Nothing more can be said about this? If the Supreme is liberated, then no one can know anything about Him. If the Supreme is bound by material nature, He is not the Supreme whatsoever. To further expound upon this passage, Vijñāna Bhikṣu, a Sāṅkhya commentator, states:

Nanv evam īśvara-pratipādaka-śrutīnāṁ kā gatis tatrāha: "What is the purport of the Vedic passages which declare the existence of the Supreme Lord? In ***Kapila-sutra, 1.96***, that explanation is provided. It is ***muktātmanaḥ praśaṁsā upāsāsiddhasya vā:*** 'The descriptions of a 'Supreme Lord' in the Vedic literature are really only the glorifications or worship of liberated souls.'"

In this way, Sāṅkhya states that the Supreme Lord does not exist.

Nyāya: This is the philosophy proposed by Gautama, wherein he asserts ***pramāṇa-prameya-saṁśaya-prayojana-dṛṣṭānta-siddhāntāvayava-tarka-nirṇaya-vāda-jalpa-vitaṇḍā-hetv- ābhāsa-chala-jāti-nigraha-sthānānāṁ tattva-jñānān niḥśreyasādhigamaḥ:*** "One attains the greatest good by studying all the different branches of Logic, viz., pramāṇa, prameya, saṁśaya, prayojana, dṛṣṭānta, siddhānta, avayava, tarka, nirṇaya, vāda, jalpa, vitaṇḍā, hetu, ābhāsa, chala, and jāti-nigraha."

What is this "greatest benefit" of which Gautama speaks? I cannot see it. Perhaps, he proposes that expertise in the knowledge of Logic is a great boon for the living entities. Amongst the above-mentioned sixteen items that he claims bring great benefit, the Supreme is not included. That is the reason the Vedas affirm the aphorism ***naiṣā tarkeṇa matir apaneyā:*** "The Supreme cannot be comprehended by material logic."

Gautama's perspective on liberation is ***duḥkha-janma-pravṛtti-doṣa-mithyā-jñānānām uttarottarāpāye tad-anantarāpāyād apavargaḥ:*** "That ultimate and unlimited freedom is the attainment of knowledge, which liberates one from the false and evil wellspring of miseries."

As a general rule, this sūtra is seen to support the misconception that liberation is merely the cessation of miseries. In Gautama's idea of liberation, spiritual bliss in not to be found. According to his theory, there can be no bliss from the contact of the Supreme Lord. This is the reason that Gautama's Nyaya is opposed to the Vedas. That concludes our depiction of his philosophy.

Vaiśeṣika: There is no need to consider a lengthy analysis of this philosophy promulgated by Kaṇāda. It is stated in his sūtras that there is no eternal Supreme Lord. Some who compose their work in his tradition include the Supersoul, residing within the body of the conditioned soul, to be one of the seven foundational principles of existence. These authors, however, made no effort to force out the atheism inherent in their philosophy.

In their commentaries on Vedanta-sutra, Śaṅkara and other pandits consider Kaṇāda's philosophy both anti-Vedic and atheistic. The reality is that any philosophy that does not accept the Supreme as the independent Creator, and instead proposes some other misconception, is, in fact, atheism. The svarūpa or intrinsic nature of the Supreme is that He is the Master of everyone and everything. Any presentation that allows some other entity to be equal to the Supreme is atheism.

Jaimini: The author of the karma-mīmāṁsā-sūtras did not write about the Supreme; his chief topic was pious action. He stated ***codanā-lakṣaṇo 'rtho dharmaḥ karmaike tatra darśanāt:*** "The Vedas teach the religion of good karma, pious action." The commentator on the karma-mīmāṁsā-sūtras, Swāmī Śabara, asks ***kathaṁ punar idam avagamyate asti tad apūrvam:*** "How to understand this? It is understood by means of the apūrva. Good karma or pious action is performed in the beginning. Then, from those deeds, an abstract, secondary principle, the apūrva, becomes manifest. It is the apūrva which gives the results of pious action. Why is there any need for a Supreme Lord to give such results?"

Modern atheists and Comte have no power to propagate anything more outrageous than this.

The Vedānta-sūtra promulgates only devotional service to the Supreme. In their commentaries on it, many atheists preached the Advaita philosophy of impersonalism, which is nothing more than covered Buddhism. Nevertheless, in order to show mankind the true path of liberation, devoted saints have scrutinizingly written accurate commentaries on Vedānta-sūtra. Later in our book, we shall explain why the philosophy of Advaita impersonalism is completely wrong.

Pātañjala-śāstra is another name for the ***Yoga-śāstra***, written by Patañjali Rishi. In its Sādhana-khāṇḍa, a sūtra is found which reads ***kleśa-karma-vipākāśayair aparāmṛṣṭaḥ puruṣa-viśeṣa īśvaraḥ tatra niratiśayaṁ sārvajña-bījam sa tu purveṣām api guruḥ kālenānavacchedāt:*** "The Omniscient Supreme Controller is untouched by misery, karmic reaction, destiny, or calamity. Because time cannot touch him, he is the master of everything."

Reading this description of the Supreme, many people may consider Patañjali to be a true devotee. At the end of the Yoga-śāstra, however, such an erroneous impression is dispelled. There in the Kaivalya-pāda, Patañjali writes ***puruṣārtha-śūnyānāṁ guṇānāṁ pratiprasavaḥ kaivalyaṁ svarūpa-pratiṣṭhā vā citi-śaktir iti:*** "When the goals of religiosity, economic development, sense gratification, and liberation come to an end, then kaivalya, real liberation, thus manifests, establishing the soul's original nature."

This sūtra is further explained in the Bhoja-vṛtti as ***cic-chakter vṛtti-sārūpya-nivṛttau svarūpa-mātre 'vasthānaṁ tat kaivalyam ucyate:*** "When the soul is without form and situated in its spiritual essence, that is said to be kaivalya."

This means that kaivalya is attained when the spiritual potency is situated in its own nature. What is the meaning of "liberation of the spiritual potency" in this passage? Does it mean that the individual spirit soul no longer performs action after attaining liberation? Does it mean that the individual spirit soul continues to have a relationship with the Supreme after liberation? The Yoga-sastra, unfortunately, does not answer these queries. Pouring over it, the reader will be convinced that the "Supreme Controller" depicted in the Sādhana-khāṇḍa portion of the book is considered only an imaginary being, created in order to help the practitioner attain spiritual perfection. After attaining perfection, that idea of a Supreme Lord is no longer taken seriously. Is the Yoga-sastra theistic or atheistic? You decide.

Atheism has been preached in many different languages in many different countries in many different ways and under many different names.

karma-jñāna-vimiśrā yā yuktis tarkamayī nare /
citra-mata-prasūtī sā saṁsāra-phala-dāyinī //18//

In the world of man, logic mixed with fruitive action and philosophical speculation generates variegated ideas, delivering the fruit of repeated birth and death.

Purport

Logic is known as yukti, and it is of two kinds: Śuddha or pure and miśra or mixed. Śuddha-yukti or pure logic is present in the original, pure nature of the liberated spirit soul. His activities, however, are mixed with material ideas while he is imprisoned in material nature; he then possesses what I term miśra-yukti, or mixed logic. This also is of two kinds: Mixed with karma or fruitive action and mixed with jñana or speculative knowledge. Mixed logic is also called tarka, speculation.

It is very evil, for we see within it four defects: Mistakes, illusions, the cheating propensity, and imperfect senses. Its conclusions are always faulty. Pure logic arrives at identical conclusions, but mixed logic arrives at a great variety of mutually contradictory conclusions. By acting in accordance to the conclusions of mixed knowledge, conditioned souls in this world are more tightly bound to the prison-house of matter.

yuktes tu jaḍa-jātāyā jaḍātīte na yojanā /
ato jaḍāśritā yuktir vadaty evaṁ pralāpanam //19//

But that logic, born of and taking shelter of dull matter, is unable to go beyond matter. Thus, it utters ridiculous words.

Purport

Mixed logic emanates from dull matter. Through the perceptions of the doors of the senses, the conditioned soul gets a glimpse of material images. This glimpse is carried by the nerves to the brain. The power of memory preserves them in the brain, and then mixed logic goes to work. A great variety of imaginary ideas are thus created. Mixed logic sorts through these images, arranging them in attractive patterns; this is then called philosophy and science. When mixed logic analyzes these sensory images in this way and that, it comes to some definitive conclusion. This is called reason.

Comte advises us: "With diligence and care, organize and preserve all you have seen. Then, examine that information in order to discern the truth." Mixed logic can understand something of the material world by examining the images experienced through material sense perception. Why should it not be then called material logic? How can such material logic hope to know the nature and activities of that which is beyond this material world? If there is indeed something that exists beyond this world, then there must also exist a specific process to understand it. When an uneducated brute takes shelter of only material logic--without cognizance of the spiritual process for attaining real knowledge and not wanting to know that such a process even exists--then he will talk nonsense only. How can there be any doubt about this?

Material logic only brings good results when targeted toward understanding the way in which the material world works. Mixed logic is quite suitable for music, warfare, medicine, engineering, and similar activities. At first, material logic is mixed with speculation, jñāna-miśra-yukti. In this theoretical stage, the scientist comes to know general principles. Then comes the second stage, wherein such theoretical knowledge is applied in order to solve practical problems; that is known as karma-miśra-yukti.

As an example, take the building of a railroad. First there is the theoretical stage and, after that, the application stage, where the railroad is actually constructed. Engineering and other similar activities are the conventional sphere for mixed logic, but that which is beyond matter is not its proper sphere.

Mixed logic cannot comprehend the world beyond matter; that is not its proper sphere. Only spiritual logic can understand that world. Materialism or the worship of material nature, Nirvāṇa, and Skepticism take shelter of material logic in order to understand the original cause of this material world, although that cause is beyond matter. Such an application for such a purpose will never deliver a joyful result, and that's the reason that these philosophies are a laughing-stock. The books that these logicians have written are only so much ridiculous babble.

pralapantīha sā yuktir udantī svātma-siddhaye /
carame parameśānaṁ svī-karoti bhayāturā //20//

Here in this world, that logic speaks nonsense. For its own self-perfection, filled with fear, at the end it accepts the Supreme Lord.

Purport

Pure logic is a natural gift to spirit soul. Nevertheless, when he is bound in the material world, spirit soul, continuously meditating upon matter, considers mixed logic to be superior. Most people are, in this way, adherents of mixed logic. Knowing the mysteries of service to the Supreme, and knowing the glories of fixed concentration upon the Supreme, only the fortunate souls appreciate pure logic.

Hoping to achieve their own selfish desires, people here have venerated mixed logic for a very long time. They gave the concepts of material logic great esteem. However, at the end, these people were unable to find happiness.

Mixed or material logic does not leave the conditioned soul, but, sometimes, material logic turns out to assist the soul. In contending with a cornucopia of philosophies while speaking in various ways, mixed logic could not find happiness. Then it began to hate itself. Chattering over and over, material logic lamented and grieved. It proclaimed: "Alas! How long I have worked hard here in this material world? I have, rejecting my own true nature, fallen very far away from my eternal associate, my real self, spirit soul."

In the end, grieving again and again like this—and now loaded with various fears—material logic acquiesces to the Supreme, accepting Him as the original cause of all causes.

The mixed preaching about the Supreme, born from the mind of man and material logic, can be found in country after country. In his book Kusumāñjali, Udayanācārya depicted this idea. Known as Deism or Natural Theology in Europe and the West—and having a certain kind of popularity there--this barren belief in the Supreme has issued forth from many minds. When theism is established by mixed logic, such incomplete knowledge of the Supreme is most imperfect.

The reason for this is that material logic is extremely weak, having no qualification to bring spirit closer to the Supreme. It cannot elevate the conditioned soul, because it is against the intrinsic nature of the spirit self. Material knowledge is unable to deliver spiritual knowledge or actually guide the spirit soul, and that will be shown later in our treatise.

kadācid īśa-tattve sā jaḍa-bhrānta-pralāpinī /
dvaitaṁ traitaṁ bahutvaṁ vāropayaty eva yatnataḥ //21//

Sometimes, with effort, bewildered by dull matter and speaking nonsense about the Supreme, it (mixed logic) imagines one or two or many (Supreme Lords).

Purport

Sometimes, mixed logic may accept the existence of the Supreme. Nevertheless, confused by matter and always babbling, this logic is unable to accept only one Supreme. At times, mixed logic speculates that there must be two. Then it contemplates the idea that there is a good Supreme but also a separate material Supreme. The Divine Spirit brings benefic things, and the other Supreme brings distresses. A speculative philosopher of the name Zarathustra preached this concept of two Supremes. In his book, the Zendavesta, he professed that these two were both eternal entities.

It was by the influence of Zarathustra's ideas that Satan, an equally-powerful rival to the Supreme, made his imaginary appearance first in the religion of the Jews and then in the religion of the Koran. Those who are actually devoted to the Supreme are simply contemptuous of these old concoctions. Similarly, they are contemptuous of atheistic jñāna-kāṇḍa and karma-kāṇḍa philosophies. Zarathustra is a philosopher from antiquity. When his speculation was not at all respected in India, he pushed it in Persia.

After that, influenced by his concept of two Supremes, the theory of three Gods—a so-called Trinity—emerged in a belief system that had initially sprung from the religion of the Jews. In the beginning, these three were all considered Supreme Lords. However, when its philosophers became disenchanted with that concept, the Trinity transformed into God, Christ, and the Holy Ghost. In India, contemporary to this development, a very ridiculous idea emerged, wherein Brahmā, Viṣṇu, and Śiva were considered competing Supremes.

Some speculative philosophers then promulgated the misconception that these three are actually all only one Supreme Lord; indeed, many portions of Vedic literature proscribe the idea that we should consider them separate, independent, or competing Lords. Faith in concurrent and different Supreme Lords is seen in many other countries. Indeed, amongst countries of the worst rank of civilization, it is hard to uncover pure faith in one Supreme. There are times when Indra, Candra, Vāyu, as well as others, are thought to be independent, competitor Gods.

Different philosophers disproved that erroneous concept and authenticated that only Brahman is the Supreme. The speculations of many Gods are nothing more than idiot chatter from an ordinary logic perplexed by matter. There is only One Supreme Lord. If there were more than one, this world would not be as well organized as it is. If there were many independent and rival Controllers, They would decree separate and conflicting laws of material nature, as per Their individual desires. There is no doubt about this. An intelligent and introspective person, when analyzing this material world, can only conclude that it was created in accordance to the Will of One Supreme Controller.

jñānaṁ sāhajikaṁ hitvā yuktir na vidyate kvacit /
kathaṁ sā parame tattve taṁ hitvā sthātum arhati //22//

Nowhere is there any real logic separate from the natural knowledge of the spirit soul. Abandoning that, how can anyone establish the Supreme Absolute Truth?

Purport

Logic which emanates from the natural knowledge of the spirit soul is pure and without fault. Philosophy produced by that logic is real Truth, but so-called true logic is unable to stand when separated from natural knowledge. Logic that emanates from material knowledge, however, is the logic seen everywhere in this world; it is forever mixed and impure. Philosophies that emanate from such mixed logic are ever full of fault and insufficient. Such philosophies are never proficient at describing the Supreme. Mixed knowledge is not the appropriate tool for describing the Supreme Absolute Truth.

The appropriate tool for describing the Supreme Absolute Truth is pure logic, taking shelter of spirit soul's intrinsic knowledge. Here, a person may query: "What is this natural knowledge about which you speak?" The answer is that original knowledge possessed by the spirit soul is termed here as "natural knowledge." He is all-spiritual and always full of knowledge. Natural knowledge is eternally present in spirit soul and not created by the perceptions of the things of this world. The action of that natural knowledge is known as pure logic. Before the spirit soul knew anything of the material world, that natural knowledge was known by the soul.

That natural knowledge is:

1) I exist;

2) I continue to exist;
3) I'm happy;
4) My happiness emanates from a certain place, a shelter, which is the reservoir of happiness;
5) It is natural for me to seek the shelter of that reservoir;
6) I am eternally a devotee of that reservoir of all happiness;
7) That reservoir is extremely beautiful;
8) I have not the power to forsake that reservoir;
9) My current condition is deplorable;
10) Abandoning this deplorable condition, I should again take shelter of that reservoir of happiness;
11) This material world is not my eternal abode;
12) Elevation in this world does not translate into eternal elevation.

Logic remains mixed with matter if it does not take shelter of this natural knowledge. Such logic is then only nonsense twaddle. In the beginning, some first principles or axioms must be accepted, even in ordinary science. One cannot make progress in math, astronomy, or other sciences without first accepting its axioms. One must also accept some first principles in understanding the spiritual science—the axioms of natural knowledge. Those first principles are the root from which the tree of spiritual knowledge flourishes.

ekatvam api tad dṛṣṭvā tat-samādhi-cchalena ca /
sthūlaṁ bhittvā tu liṅge sā yogāśraya-caraty aho //23//

Supposedly seeing that oneness, on the pretense of rapt concentration and breaking through (the barricade) of gross matter--although still on the astral plane—he, alas, goes to take shelter of yoga.

Purport

Some speculative philosophers reject belief in the soul's natural knowledge, but they also do not fully believe in material logic. Others, accepting the concept of spirit soul's natural knowledge, profess faith in one Supreme Lord. They take shelter of what appears to be a samādhi—one filled with a variety speculations--but their trance in meditation is not real. It is a deception only. In their simulation of meditation, they pretend to break through the barriers enclosing the gross world of matter, and they then feign seeing the spiritual world.

Why is their meditation nothing more than counterfeit? That is because the world of spirit is revealed only through authentic trance. There is no such revelation in the pretense of trance. They think that they have seen the ultimate abode of spirit and spiritual entities, but they are seeing only the astral world of matter, the world of thoughts. They have, in truth, taken shelter in this subtle world only.

The gross material world and the subtle material world are different, and that difference is explained in this way: Gross matter is perceived by the gross material senses, and subtle matter is perceived by the mind. Subtle matter manifested first, before gross matter. As such, the material world is partitioned into these two, viz. the world of gross material elements and the subtle and effulgent world of thoughts. The astral body of the Theosophists is an effulgent material body consisting of thoughts; it is called mind. The splendorous, subtle world described in Patañjali's Yoga-śāstra—and also found in Buddhist philosophy—is nevertheless nothing more than the subtle material world of thoughts.

Different from this is the spiritual world. It is different from the gross world, different from the astral world, and also different from the liberation called kaivalya in Patañjali's Yoga-śāstra. The Yoga-śāstra does not depict the spiritual world. In its practices, that śāstra explicitly depicts a soul and a relationship with the Supreme. In its description of liberation, however, the Yoga-śāstra makes no mention of the Supreme nor of the liberated soul's eternal relationship with Him. If, indeed, the motive is that individual souls and the Supreme have then merged as one, that philosophy of yoga is non-different from Monism.

The philosophy of Yoga-śāstra delineated by Patañjali does not deliver eternal auspiciousness to any spirit souls. It may be considered one of many such philosophies that remain in between the world of matter and the world of spirit. That is the reason that sincere souls searching after real spiritual happiness do not like it.

kecid vadanti viśvaṁ vai pareśa-nirmitaṁ kila /
jīvānāṁ sukha-bhogāya dharmāya ca viśeṣataḥ //24//

Some say the universe was indeed created by the Supreme Lord for variegated material happiness of the conditioned souls, as well as pious religious activity of those souls.

Purport

Some philosophers contend that the Supreme created this universe as a chance to enjoy sense gratification. Then, after enjoying these over and over, free from sin, we are meant perform pious acts in order to attain His mercy. If the Godhead actually created this material world for the conditioned soul's enjoyment, however, He would not have constructed it with so many faults. When all is said and done, He is omnipotent; whatever He desires is enacted immediately. If He had designed it for the pleasure of the conditioned soul, He would have created it without faults.

If it was created by Him for the purpose of the conditioned souls executing pious action, He would have made it much different from the way it is. There can be no doubt about this. Why can there be no doubt? The reason is that, here in this world, pious deeds are not readily or easily executed by every living being.

ādi-jīvāparādhād vai sarveṣāṁ bandhanaṁ dhruvam /
tathānya-jīva-bhūtasya vibhor daṇḍena niṣkṛtiḥ //25//

(Others contend that) due to the original human offense, there must be irrevocable imprisonment for everyone after that. Later, by punishment of Himself, God enables deliverance for conditioned souls (who follow Him).

Purport

Some monotheists absorbed in their version of morality, considering the virtues and evils of this world, concluded that this is not a place of uncontaminated enjoyment, that miseries outweigh pleasures here. They concluded that it is a place of imprisonment meant to punish the conditioned souls. Since there is punishment here, there must have been some kind of crime; if there was no such crime, why would there be any punishment? What was that crime which the conditioned souls committed?

These monotheists, men of meager intelligence, unable to answer this question in a logical manner, produced a very wild speculation. The Supreme is said to have created an original man and put him in a nice garden, along with his wife. Then, He prohibited him from tasting the fruit of the knowledge tree there. Complying, however, with a wicked suggestion from an evil being, the original man and his wife tasted the fruit of the knowledge tree, and, therefore, defied the order of the Supreme Lord. Accordingly, they fell from that nice garden into a material sphere, a world full of miseries. Due to that original offense, all other living beings also are offenders from the time they take birth.

The Supreme, unable to envision any way to eradicate this original offense, took birth in the human form. He then took the sins of all of His followers and died as a result. Anyone who follows Him easily attains emancipation, but all those who do not follow Him fall into an eternal hell. In this way, the Supreme assumes what appears to be a human form, punishes and executes His Own Self, and, in doing so, liberates His adherents. No intelligent man or woman can make any sense of this.

janmato jīva-sambhāvo maraṇānte na janma vai /
yat-kṛtaṁ saṁsṛtau tena jīvasya caramaṁ phalam //26//

(They go on to say that) the soul manifests at birth and, at the end, dies. There is indeed no rebirth. What is done in this world during a sole birth (produces) that final result for the living being.

Purport

In order to accept such a bewildered religion, a person must, from the very beginning, believe the following implausible ideas: The soul's life begins at birth and ends at death. He did not exist before his birth. After his death, the soul will no longer remain in a material world of external activities. Only humans have souls; other creatures do not.

Only those with utmost dull intellect believe in this religion. The living entity is not originally spiritual in this belief system. The Supreme created living beings from matter according to His own will. Why are they born in very different stations and situations? The followers of this religion have no reasonable explanation.

Why is one human born in a house full of miseries, another born in one full of joy, another born in one owned by a believer in the Supreme, and another born in the house of an evil atheist? Why does one person, born in an environment where he is encouraged to perform pious acts, perform them and become good? Why is another born in an environment where he is encouraged to engage in sin, does so, and then becomes evil? The adherents of this religion are unable to answer any of these questions. It seems that their religion is inferring that the Supreme is both unfair and unreasonable.

Why do they claim that beasts are without souls? Why do not the birds and the beasts have souls just as humans have? Why are humans afforded only one life here, and, as a result of their actions in that spot life, are eternally rewarded in heaven or eternally punished in hell? For anyone who has faith in a truly compassionate and merciful Supreme Lord, this religion is utterly unacceptable.

atra sthitasya jīvasya karma-jñānānuśīlanāt /
viśvonnati-vidhānena kartavyam īśa-toṣaṇam //27//

Through improvements in the world, by cultivating fruitive action and mental speculation, the good work accomplished here (through this work) by the conditioned souls makes the Supreme Lord satisfied.

Purport

The adherents of this religion do not have the power to selflessly worship the Supreme. Their general idea is that, by nurturing fruitive action and mental speculative philosophy, one should labor to make improvements in this world; in this way, they automatically please the Supreme. By many different kinds of philanthropic activities, such as building schools and hospitals, they attempt to do good for the world and, in this way, please the Lord.

Worship of the Supreme Lord through the performance of karma and jñāna are most important to them. They are unable to comprehend pure devotional service, śuddha-bhakti, which is free from karma and jñāna. Worship of the Supreme, out of a sense of duty to the world, can never be either unselfish or natural: "He has been kind to us, so we must worship Him."

These are ideas of lesser minds.

Why is this mentality not a good way to worship the Supreme? The reason is that a person may then think, "If He is not kind to me, then I shall not worship Him." With such a mentality, he has the selfish and evil desire that he must always secure the Supreme's future material kindness. However, if a person hopes for the kindness from Him that allows the soul to serve Him, then there is no fault in it. Nevertheless, the religion under discussion here does not see it like that. This religion views His kindness in terms of a person's enjoyment of a happy life here.

īśa-rūpa-vihīnas tu sarvago vidhi-sevitaḥ /
pūjito 'tra bhavaty eva prārthanā-vandanādibhiḥ //28//

But (others contend) the Supreme is all-pervading and without form, only worshipped here through service executed under scriptural regulation, beginning with prayers and obeisances.

Purport

In modern times, and appearing in many versions, the adherents of this philosophy claim that the Supreme is without form and is all-pervading. Philosophical speculation is the utmost important activity of these people. "Those who contend that the Supreme has form are stunted midgets." This idea constantly runs through their minds. "According to our path of knowledge, we understand that the Supreme is all-pervading and formless." They cannot transcend these kinds of thought.

Thinking that the Supreme is like the material sky, all-pervading and formless, the unintelligent people on this path have the conception that worship of the form of the Supreme is ridiculous idolatry. Thus, the object of their worship remains material.

The individual spirit soul is beyond the twenty-four elements of material creation. Beyond the spirit soul is the Supreme, Who has infinite qualities, Who has spiritual form, Who is all-pervading, and Whose true nature differs from the formless Supreme of the impersonalists' imagination. He is the Supreme Master, Who is supremely merciful, Who is the individual spirit soul's true friend, Who has all opulence, Who is the Supreme Controller, and Whose beautiful, transcendental form the adherents of impersonalism are without the power to envision or to even comprehend.

Their worship of the Supreme is incomplete and full of faults; it consists of merely bowing down and reciting prayers. Due to simply bowing down and reciting prayers, their form of worship is quite material in nature. Over and over, chewing the chewed of varying types of philosophical speculation, they are most fearful of worshipping the spiritual and glorious Deity form of the Supreme, to become His servant and completely surrendered to Him. Disturbed like this, they espouse to everyone in the world that no one should ever imagine a spiritual form of the Supreme.

They maintain that the worship of the Deity form of the Supreme is an adoration of what is merely a statue consisting of material elements. They have not the power to comprehend the true from of the Supreme, a form that is beyond contact with matter, that is eternal, full of knowledge, and blissful. Each of these impersonalists thinks himself to be the best and most important man.

They proclaim that it is an evil idea to take shelter at the feet of a bona fide guru. Due to fear, they will not search out a bona fide saint or spiritual master. They will not serve in devotion the lotus feet of such a spiritual master. Fearful that they will contact an imposter—and, by him, be initiated upon the wrong path—they neglect even genuine and saintly spiritual masters.

Amongst them, some say that, by one's own effort, a person can find the ultimate spiritual truth within his own heart. Therefore, there is no requirement of taking shelter of the lotus feet of a spiritual master. There are also others amongst them who say that one should simply accept only the most prominent, the most famous, spiritual master, calling him the pradhāna-ācārya: "The most famous guru is the Supreme Himself, and He is the real teacher and protector. He enters our hearts and destroys the sins within us. There is no need whatsoever to accept some human as guru."

Others amongst them contend that one should only worship the scriptures given by the Supreme. Then again, still others amongst them claim that those scriptures are full of mistakes; due to this fear, they will not agree to honor any scripture.

idam eva mataṁ viddhi sarvatraivāsamañjasam /
īśvare doṣadaṁ sākṣāt jīvasya kṣaudra-sādhakam //29//

Know that this opinion is certainly wrong in all respects. It directly impugns faults onto the Supreme Lord. It is of little help to the conditioned soul.

Purport

Although belief in one Absolute Truth rests in it, in many places this philosophy is erroneous. It implies that the Supreme is both unjust and vicious. Considering them unimportant, this philosophy also slights the devotees who are eager to serve the Supreme. He is one and is always a person. It is due to His supreme will that individual spirit souls are endowed with their own free will, and, accordingly, may choose to sin. Doing so, and thus giving up their own original nature, they are powerless in confronting the Māyā-śakti of the Supreme. Therefore, they become weak spiritually and engage in sin.

As such, the sins of the individual, conditioned souls all issue forth from weakness. If someone says that piety and sin are not beginningless, then that person must also believe that the Supreme is at fault for creating individual souls weak, prone to engage in sin. Although by lips they say that the Supreme is without fault, actually they hurl insults at Him, inferring that He has many faults.

These people are without the power to discriminate between the spirit soul and gross and subtle material coverings of the soul. They are contaminated and stunted in their theoretical knowledge, as well as their practical application of knowledge. For this reason, they are without power to comprehend the intrinsic nature and mysteries of spirit soul. Despite being very proud of their material knowledge, their actual knowledge of spirit is stunted, and their religious activities deliver only meager results. Their topmost goal is to reside in Svargaloka in their astral bodies. Therefore, they are without the power to distinguish soul from mind.

kecid vadanti sarvaṁ yac cid-acid-īśvarādikam /
brahma sanatanaṁ sākṣād ekam evādvitīyakam //30//

Some say that what is spirit, matter, the Supreme, and everything else is directly the eternal brahmajyoti only, one without a second.

Purport

The Advaita philosophy, Monism or impersonalism, has been extant since antiquity. This philosophy was derived from a very few isolated passages in Vedic literature. There is no doubt that it originated in India, although it has been spread, by various philosophers, in many countries of the world.

Arriving in India, some men of learning who accompanied Alexander the Great there, assimilated this impersonal philosophy, returned to their country, and then incorporated parts of it in their books. This impersonalism espouses: "Impersonal brahman is all that exists and nothing else. The conception of spirit, matter, and a Supreme Controller, as being different entities, is useful for ordinary activities alone.

In reality, they have all grown from brahman, the changeless root. It is eternal, without form, without change, and without qualities. It has no characteristics, no power, and no activities. It never transforms into anything else. All these statements can be found in different sections of the Vedas."

The impersonalists believe all of these ideas.

Nevertheless, taking a look around the material world—a world that is full of variety--they considered, "How is it possible that the origin of this world is impersonal brahman? We see this world with our own eyes. How did this variegated world come into existence? Our philosophy will have no endurance if we are unable to answer these questions."

Pondering upon this over and over, they deliberated upon these points: "We know that brahman at no time performs any action, so how could it have created the world? How can we accept the notion that it has such power to act? If we accept the idea that there is something else other than brahman, our whole Advaita-vāda will be shattered." Pondering upon it again and again, they arrived at the following conclusion: "If we say that brahman does have the power to transform itself into other things, that will not dismantle our Advaita-vāda. As such, brahman transformed itself into the things of this world. We can believe in that."

vastunaḥ parimāṇād vā vivarta-bhāvataḥ kila /
jagad-vicitratā sādhyā jagad anyaṁ na vartate //31//

In reality, universal variety certainly attains from the state of transformation (of brahman) or from the state of an illusion. The universe is nothing other than this.

Purport

The theory of transformation was accepted in this way. However, another impersonalist then said, "It is incorrect to say that brahman is defective, as it no longer remains brahman when transformed. As such, this theory of transformation must be cast very far away, and the theory of illusion should be accepted instead and put into its place.

The brahman never at any time transforms into any other thing, and, thus, the theory of transformation is an impossibility. However, my theory maintains that everything in existence is, in reality, brahman and only brahman; the misconception that variety exists is an illusion. My theory is a beautiful one, in every limb. When someone mistakes a rope for a snake, he becomes fearful. When someone mistakes a shining seashell for silver, he becomes filled with hope.

Thus, if my theory of illusion is accepted, then brahman is without defect. This material world is an illusion, and it is only due to ignorance that anyone believes that it exists. It is in this way that my theory is proved. Neither the material world nor life actually exists; only brahman exists. The belief that the material world really exists is only a pretending on the part of brahman. This pretension is assigned terms such as avidyā, māyā, and other words that can be found in dictionaries. This pretending here does not mean that there is something in existence that is different from brahman.

Thus, brahman is the sole reality, and nothing else exists. The reality is spirit; the pretending or illusion is matter. That has now been proved. When material consciousness is overcome by this spiritual truth, then material pretension is annihilated, actual reality revealed, and liberation is thus attained."

athavā jīva-cintāyāṁ jātaṁ sarvaṁ jagad dhruvam /
jīveśvare na bhedo 'sti jīvaḥ sarveśvareśvaraḥ //32//

Then again (others claim) all that is situated in this world is born of the ideation of the soul. The soul is the controller. There is no difference whatsoever between the soul and the Supreme Lord of all.

Purport

Other philosophers also consider another particular theory of pretension to be true. They say: "This pretending--that there is a separate material world—does not manifest from nothing. First, brahman pretends that it is an individual soul. Then it pretends that there is a separate material world that actually exists. How is it possible for some kind of so-called individual soul to be separate from brahman? It is not possible. If it is promulgated that the soul is different from brahman, then our impersonalist philosophy will be immediately destroyed. The individual soul is, therefore, the pretension of brahman."

In due course of time, these speculators divided into two groups, with two differing philosophies. The first group maintains that: "The brahman is like the great sky, and the individual soul, covered by illusion, is like a small portion of sky within a pot of clay. When brahman is cut by ignorance into small pieces, those pieces are each the individual soul. As such, the soul and brahman are different."

The second group disputes this, saying, "This conception is an embarrassment to brahman. It claims that brahman can be cut into pieces and overcome by illusion. The actual truth is not like that, however. Please understand that the individual soul is a reflection of brahman, like the sun or moon reflected on water. The soul as an individual is an illusion. By him, this deceptive world of matter is imagined to exist. In reality, brahman alone exists and nothing but brahman. The individual soul is non-different from brahman. The material world is also non-different from brahman."

There is a very great blunder reposited in both of these philosophies, a mistake that these speculators, rendered blind by thoughtless loyalty to their own concoctions, have no power or desire to see. The blunder is the misconception that brahman alone exists, and there is nothing other than brahman. If they do not accept that Brahman has powers that are inconceivable, then all their conceptions are worth nothing. Some speak of māyā or illusion, others speak of avidyā or ignorance, others talk about pretending, and still others talk about pretending to pretend. However, if they maintain that Brahman is without the power to do anything, then how can they establish their contention that nothing other than brahman exists?

This fatal flaw is seen in each and every one of their contentions, and it destroys the impersonalist philosophy. If we say that Brahman alone exists, and if we accept that Brahman has inconceivable power, then Brahman is not required to take shelter of anything except Brahman. As such, Brahman is non-different from any power or substance. Accordingly, Brahman's inconceivable, contradictory powers—power to change and changelessness, power to be formless but to also have form, power to have both qualities and be without them--can eternally and simultaneously exist, along with many other mutually contradictory natures within Brahman, without negating the existence of each other.

Even the topmost effort of human reasoning is unable to understand Brahman's inconceivable power.

Brahman has inconceivable power. Why should we not accept this Truth? Having inconceivable powers, the glories of Brahman are greater than the glory of the impersonal brahman, which is without qualities. I glorify the Param Brahman, the Supreme Brahman. That Brahman Who has transcendental powers is the Supreme Brahman. The brahman that is without qualities or powers is merely termed brahman. That brahman is only a part of the Supreme Brahman.

The philosophy that accepts only this partial brahman--and turns away from the Supreme Brahman--is a most inferior kind of philosophy, one born of small intelligences. There is no doubt about that. This philosophy of impersonalism is without the power to answer questions posed to it by solid logic. It is without the power to know the true meaning of the Vedas. It has no power to deliver the greatest auspiciousness to individual, spirit souls.

eteṣu vāda-jāleṣu tat sad eva viniścitam /
anvaya-vyatirekābhyām advaya-jñānaṁ eva yat //33//

That eternal (knowledge), which is certainly one, can be both directly and indirectly understood for certain somewhere within this labyrinth of so many philosophies.

Purport

All these different philosophies are like a labyrinthine net, shabbily woven by different philosophers. Within all these conflicting philosophies, the Truth is to be located somewhere. Casting all of the untruths away and discovering the actual Truth is known as "finding the Truth." A French philosopher of the name Victor Kunja attempted to understand the Truth in this way. In the end, however, he was unable to discover it. The reason he failed was that he searched only within the thinking of Western philosophers.

Western intelligence is extremely materialistic. Western philosophers were without the power to comprehend the difference between what is spirit soul and what is not spirit. Their minds remain firmly fixed in attachment to matter. They claim that the material mind is the spirit soul. Just as looking for grains of rice amongst the empty husks of threashed rice can bring no fruitful result, similarly, Victor Kunja's search, in the end, bore no fruit.

In Mantra Fifteen of ***Śrī Īśopaniṣad***, it is stated:

hiraṇmayena pātreṇa satyasāphihitaṁ mukham
tat tvaṁ pūṣann apāvṛṇu satya-dharmaya-dṛṣṭaye

"By the golden, dazzling effulgence of the Absolute effulgence, Your face is covered. O Sustainer of all that lives, kindly remove that covering in order to exhibit Yourself to Your pure devotee."

In Śrīmad-Bhāgavatam (11.8.10), it is said ***aṇubhyaś ca bṛhadbhyaś ca śāstrebhyaḥ kuśalo naraḥ sarvataḥ sāram ādadyāt puṣpebhya iva ṣaṭpadaḥ:***

"Just as the bee takes honey from all flowers big and small, an intelligent man should take the essence from all books, both great and small."

In this way, Vaiṣṇava philosophers discover Truth in scriptures like the Vedas and Bhāgavat. The Vaiṣṇava discovers the Absolute Truth in the very important books, which explain the science of the spirit soul, and in the less-important books, written by materialistic philosophers. Part of that Truth is known as advaya-jñāna, knowledge of the impersonal brahman. That impersonal brahman is but a small portion of the complete Supreme Absolute Truth, the Truth which is eternal, full of knowledge and bliss.

The Truth of the Supreme is described by the word ***sat***. When that ***sat*** or Truth is manifest, then the ***asat*** or untruth is cast far away. This word *sat* also refers to the spiritual world. The material world, which is only a reflection of the spiritual world, is known as ***asat***.

Thus end the Bhaktivinode purports to the First Chapter of ***Tattva-viveka,*** entitled ***Realization of Eternity.***

Chapter Two

Dvitīyānubhava: Second Realization

Realization of Eternal Consciousness

sac-cid-ānanda-sāndrāṅgaṁ parānanda-rasāśrayam /
cid-acic-chakti-sampannaṁ taṁ vande kali-pāvanam //1//

I offer my obeisances unto Him, Śrī Kṛṣṇa Caitanya Mahāprabhu, the purifier of Kali-yuga, the concentrated form of eternity, knowledge, and bliss, the shelter of supreme, nectarean joy endowed with full control of all material and spiritual potencies.

svarūpam āsthito hy ātmā svarūpa-śakti-vṛttitaḥ /
vadaty eva nijātmānam upādhi-rahitaṁ vacaḥ //2//

Indeed, the soul situated in his own form, by the power of his own spiritual nature, utters true words that certainly come from his own self, free from all material designation.

Purport

The conditioned souls, imprisoned in the material universe and influenced by matter in a variety of ways, provide many answers to the questions initially posed at the beginning of the First Chapter. The liberated souls, who know the truth of spirit soul by spiritual realization and a true understanding the teachings of the bona fide spiritual master, provide accurate answers to those questions. Each of these questions has only one correct answer. The three questions posed in the second verse of Chapter One are:

1) As he who perceives this world, who am I?
2) What is this labyrinthine world of matter?
3) What is my relationship to it?

The conditioned souls under the influence of this material nature provide a great many answers to these three questions, and those answers were delineated in Chapter One.

Now, here in the Second Chapter, the true answers to those three questions, the ones provided by self-realized souls, will be reiterated. First, however, we shall consider this particular question: Who are these self-realized souls? The self-realized souls are those without any relation to material place, time, senses, and the body; they are, instead, situated in their original spiritual nature. In the literature known as Śrīmad-Bhāgavatam, (2.10.6), a book which contains the essential teachings of Vedānta, the pure, self-realized soul is described as follows:

muktir hitvānyathā-rūpaṁ svarūpeṇa vyavasthitiḥ

"Liberation is the changeless situation, the permanent form and nature of spirit soul after he abandons ever-changing gross and subtle bodies."

When he is completely freed from material existence, the spirit soul is situated in his original form and nature. He is then truly self-realized, and that fully self-realized soul will give only correct answers to our three questions.

At this point, someone could possibly protest: "In this material world, the living entity has a body, senses, and the power of reason. If he gives up material existence, then what will happen to his body, senses, and power of reason? How will he have the power even to give correct answers to your questions?

To this protest, we answer that spirit soul is like personified spiritual knowledge. Spiritual knowledge is one of spirit soul's natural features. Spirit soul not only has spiritual knowledge of his own self, he is also filled with illumination. With the light of that knowledge, he can illuminate the features of other things as well. In this manner, the spiritual soul is in knowledge of his own self and other objects. It also means he has the power to perfectly smell, taste, see, and hear, having knowledge of his eternal nature.

The soul is shackled within a series of material sheaths when he falls into the material world. In order for him to interact with that material world, the conditioned soul is provided a second set of senses; these are material senses. In this manner, the conditioned soul sees with material eyes, hears with material ears, smells with a material nose, tastes with a material tongue, and experiences the sense of touch with material skin. His original spiritual senses then deprived of their intrinsic powers, the conditioned soul employs only powers inherent to his second set of senses, which are all material.

Furthermore, the conclusions drawn by the conditioned soul are then developed with the help of material reasoning power. This whole chain of events is a great calamity for the pure spirit soul, whose natural status is full of knowledge. When the rejuvenated soul becomes self-realized and his original nature is revived, he can once again perform all activities with his original spiritual senses. At that time, his deliberative power is once again his original and spiritual reasoning power. As such, the pure soul can provide true answers. The answers given by the self-realized soul are free from all the limitations and defects of matter.

The true answer, one which a self-realized soul residing in India provides, is also given by a self-realized soul residing in far northern countries. A liberated soul residing in the higher spiritual world of Vaikuṇṭha will give the same answer, as well. Why not? Purely liberated souls do not give answers that originate from the labyrinthine mixture of material modes, and that is why their answers are always non-different.

bhagavān eka evāste parā-śakti-samanvitaḥ /
tac-chakti-niḥsṛto jīvo brahmāṇḍaṁ ca jaḍātmakam //3//

The Supreme Personality of Godhead is certainly one. He is endowed with transcendental potency. The jīva, the material universe, and the material elements are manifest from His potency.

Purport

In Vedic literature, it is stated ***ekam evādvitīyam***: "The Supreme is one, and He is without rival."

Neha nānāsti kiñcana: "There is nothing that is separate from the Supreme."

Sa viśva-kṛd viśva-vit: "He created the universe, and He knows everything that transpires in it."

Pradhāna-kṣetra-patir guṇesaḥ: "He is the lord of the modes of nature, the material ingredients, and the material field of activities."

Eko devo bhagavān vareṇyaḥ: "There is one Supreme Lord full of all opulences, the God of all gods, and He is the greatest personality."

By these statements, the eternal existence of the Supreme Lord is confirmed with clarity. In ***Śrīmad-Bhāgavatam, (1.2.11),*** it is stated:

vadanti tat tattva-vidas tattvaṁ yaj jñānam advayam
brahmeti paramātmeti bhagavān iti śabdyate

"Those who know the Absolute Truth thus call the eternal non-dual substance brahman, Paramātmā, or Bhagavān."

The Supreme Personality of Godhead or Bhagavān is superior to both the spiritual effulgence of brahman and the all-pervasive Supersoul known as Paramātmā. Nevertheless, no one should consider that brahman or Paramātmā are two separate Supreme Lords, and that Bhagavān, the really Supreme Lord, dominates Them. Here, in this example, the individual spirit soul is the seer and Bhagavān the object seen. At the beginning of his spiritual life, when he journeys on the path of jñāna-mārga or philosophical speculation, the soul sees the brahman feature of the Supreme Personality of Godhead.

When he makes further advancement in his spiritual sojourn, the soul begins to walk the path of yoga in yoga-mārga. When he completes that, he sees the Paramātmā feature of Bhagavān. When, by great good fortune, the soul traverses the path of pure devotional service known as śuddha-bhakti-mārga, he sees Bhagavān directly. Bhagavān conveys great sweetness to his eyes. Bhagavān is full of bliss transcendental. He is eternal and full of knowledge and spiritual happiness. The form of Bhagavān is graceful, and He is a very handsome, charming personality. Bhagavān is full of all opulence, fame, beauty, knowledge, and renunciation. Bhagavān has these qualities in their best and most sublime forms.

The brahman and Paramātmā features are both hidden within Bhagavān, and He has all potencies. By His desire, His potencies manifest His continuous and occasional pastimes. Bhagavān is supremely independent, and He is the author of all rules and regulations--although they are never binding upon Him. Bhagavān is without rival, and no one is His equal. No one is ever superior to Him, and His spiritual potencies, themselves with many powers, are multifarious.

By these many and variegated potencies, Bhagavān's spiritual abode, pastimes, and paraphernalia are all manifest. All of these are transformations of Bhagavān's spiritual potency. From His perfect spiritual power, the spiritual world is manifest. Bhagavān's potency acts in multifarious ways, and one such manifestation it creates is the innumerable atoms. That is seen. The effulgence, qualities, and activities manifested from Bhagavān's spiritual potency are all spiritual.

The many jīva or individual spirit souls are all manifest from the potency known as jīva-śakti.

The spiritual potency has also a shadow, and from that shadow are manifest five gross elements, five sense objects, ten senses, the mind, the intelligence, false ego, and contaminated consciousness. Twenty-four elements of matter are manifested in this way. The shadow potency that manifests the material world is therefore designated as "chāyā-śakti."

so 'rkas tat-kiraṇo jīvo nityānugata-vigrahaḥ /
prīti-dharmaḥ cid-ātmā saḥ parānande 'pi dāya-bhāk //4//

He (Bhagavān) is like an effulgent, transcendental sun. Like a particle of that effulgence, spirit soul has an eternal form full of knowledge. Love (of Bhagavān) is the original, constitutional occupation of spirit soul. The individual spirit soul is even entitled to that highest bliss as his rightful claim.

Purport

Bhagavān is like the sun, and the individual spirit souls are like rays of light emanating from that sun. These effulgent spirit souls possess a nature similar to that of Bhagavān. Each soul has a glowing spiritual form suited to his own particular nature; each soul's form is spiritual and effulgent. Thus, each spirit soul is spiritual in nature.

Each and every spirit soul possesses spiritual qualities, and a small particle of transcendental love is part of each of their spiritual natures. Therefore, a small particle of love is intrinsic to spirit soul's nature. As such, it is said, "The soul's nature is love." Due to the form and natural love of the spirit soul being infinitesimal, it is stated that the form and love of the soul is imperfect and incomplete.

The individual spirit souls also possess a particle of spiritual bliss. The bliss attained upon realizing the impersonal brahman effulgence is described by these words in Śrīla Rūpa Gosvāmī's ***Bhakti-rasāmṛta-sindhu:***

brahmānando bhaved eṣa cet parārdha-guṇī-kṛtaḥ
naiti bhakti-sudhāmbodheḥ paramāṇu-tulām api

"Multiplied even by one-trillion, the happiness of brahmānanda is still unable to compare to the bliss derived from the ocean of śuddha-bhakti."

By his intrinsic nature, each and every individual spirit soul is qualified to inherit, like a son, the sublime, blissful, and most exalted status of śuddha-bhakti, engagement in the pure devotional service of the Supreme. Spirit soul, aware that the happiness of brahman realization is infinitesimal in comparison to that of pure devotional service, becomes Bhagavān's acolyte and servant. Śrī Bhagavān empowers the spirit soul with the powers of His higher spiritual potencies when He is pleased by a particular soul's devotional service. Then, empowered with that exalted spiritual potency, a realized soul is able to experience the sublime nectar of devotional service.

tac-chaktes chāyayā viśvaṁ sarvam etad vinirmitam /
yatra bahirmukhā jīvāḥ saṁsaranti nijecchayā //5//

This manifestation, all of these material universes, is created by a shadow of His potency. This is where conditioned souls, who have turned away their faces (from Bhagavān), wander according to their own desires.

Purport

When he is Lord Kṛṣṇa's dedicated servant, the individual spirit soul is like a son inheriting his father's property; this inheritance is his transcendental bliss. The individual spirit soul falls into the realm of repeated birth and death when he attempts to be independent, turning his face away from Lord Kṛṣṇa. The spiritual potency assists the individual spirit soul in becoming more and more spiritually elevated, but the material potency, which creates the material realm, arranges for the conditioned soul to become more rigidly shackled to the prison-house of repeated birth and death.

This material potency is the shadow of the spiritual potency. The individual soul who deserves to be sent to the realm of repeated birth and death takes his birth in that world. Once there, he is given a gross and subtle material body in order to experience a variety of perceptions within the material realm.

In this way, he falls into the material world. It is there that he suffers numerous distresses that come about as the results of his various actions or karma. These conditioned souls are in the material world for one, and only one, reason. That reason is ***bhagavad-bahirmukha***, they have turned their faces away from Bhagavān. It is understood that individual spirit souls are not manifested from the material world nor are they manifested from the higher spiritual world. They are manifested from the buffer region, a separate region between the higher spiritual sky and the rest of creation.[2]

Material pleasures may be more attractive to them than spiritual elevation. Thus, of their own free will, they may choose to remain in the realm of repeated birth and death. Bhagavān cannot be blamed for this. Displaying His mercy to these souls, Bhagavān created the material world so they could enjoy themselves there as per their desires. Bhagavān created the material realm in such a way that, after only a few days of attempting to enjoy themselves there, conditioned souls would become truly intelligent and turn away from those pleasures. In this way, Bhagavān formulated the path of executing devotional activities in the association of devoted saints. By following that path, those souls are delivered from the material world.

jīvato jaḍato vāpi bhagavān sarvadā pṛthak /
na tau bhagavato bhinnau rahasyam idam eva hi //6//

Bhagavān is at all times different from either the individual spirit soul or matter, although those two are not different from the Supreme Personality (Bhagavān). This is indeed a mystery.

Purport

Bhagavān is eternally different from the individual spirit souls and from matter, however, the spirit souls and matter are not different from Him. This is a great mystery. Through the form of

---

[2] For more on this essential topic of origination, consult Appendices One and Two.

His potency, He has entered both the individual souls and the material world. Having already made a meticulous study and revelation of all the scriptures, Vyāsadeva, unable to understand this mystery, lamented. Then the great devotee of the Lord, Śrī Devarṣī Nārada, approached Vyāsadeva and instructed him in four verses that constitute the heart of the Śrīmad-Bhāgavatam.

That heart of its teachings has been divided into four parts, and those are known as jñāna, vijñāna, rahasya, and tad-aṅga. In the jñāna section, Bhagavān instructs: "Only I am the Supreme Truth. I existed before anything else. It is I, the Personality of Godhead, the Supreme Truth, Who was existing at the beginning of the material creation, before the chain of cause and effects or the brahmajyoti were manifest in it. That which you see now is also I, the Personality of Godhead. And, after annihilation, what remains will also be I, the Personality of Godhead. When the material world is created, I manifest, by My potency, whatever then exists; when the material world is annihilated, only I shall remain."

It is in this way that Bhagavaj-jñāna is explained by Bhagavān.

In the vijñāna section, Bhagavān instructs: "Due to My potency, when conditioned souls, unable to perceive My true nature, perceive outside of Me what only appears to be of value, if it is without relation to Me, it actually has no reality. It is my Māyā. Through material perception, the way in which it is different from Me is readily seen. Know that My illusory energy is, in two ways, different from Myself: As a reflection and as darkness. When spiritually manifested, it is My Yogamāyā."

Abhāsa or reflection refers to the individual spirit souls and tamaḥ or darkness refers to the material world. This stage of knowledge is called vijñāna, knowledge of Bhagavān and His potencies. The individual spirit souls and the material world are both His potencies, and that should be understood.

In the third section known as rahasya, Bhagavān instructs: "Just as the universal elements—the pradhāna, the mahat-tattva, and the pañca-mahā-bhūta--enter into the cosmos and, at the same time, do not enter it, similarly, I Myself, the Spiritual Sun, also enter the individual spirit souls and exist within everything created. At the same time, I am outside of everything and eternally different from them. When the individual spirit soul becomes My bhakta, at that time I become his friend. That is the great secret."

In the tad-aṅga section, Bhagavān instructs: "When an individual soul, tortured by so many sufferings in this world of repeated birth and death, takes shelter at the feet of a devoted saint, he inquires from him about Absolute Truth. By his spiritual master's mercy, he then searches for Me, the Supreme Absolute Truth, the Personality of Godhead, in all circumstances, in all space and time, both directly and indirectly. He eventually attains Me."

It is in this way that the reality of acintya-bhedābheda-tattva, inconceivable oneness and difference, is explained in the Śrīmad-Bhāgavatam.

jaḍa-jāla-gatā jīvā jaḍāsaktiṁ vihāya ca /
svakīya-vṛttim ālocya śanakair labhate param //7//

By abandoning the trap of dead matter and all attachment to it, the conditioned soul engages in his own carefully considered action. Gradually, he attains the Supreme.

Purport

Individual spirit souls are divided into two groups: Those immemorially imprisoned in the material world and those free from that imprisonment. The eternally liberated souls are forever attracted to serve the Supreme Personality of Godhead, Lord Kṛṣṇa.

When conditioned souls, captured in the trap of material life, abandon their attachment to matter and go on to, with meticulous attention, execute spiritual action, they eventually attain the Supreme. Devotional service to Bhagavān is what is meant here by spiritual action. As that individual favorably executes devotional service, his attachment for material things gradually diminishes.

When those spiritual actions are perfectly complete, at that time, attachment for material things is perfectly and completely removed. Then the individual spirit soul attains the lotus feet of

Bhagavān, the Supreme Absolute Truth, the Supreme Lord of the spiritual world. In the process of repeatedly executing spiritual activities, the devotee gradually realizes them to be ever-sweeter. Conditioned souls remain averse to spirit to the extent of their material attachment.

cintātītam idaṁ tattvaṁ dvaitādvaita-svarūpakam /
caitanya-caraṇāsvādāc chuddha-jīve pratīyate //8//

This Truth (the Supreme) is beyond thought and mind, of a nature that is different and non-different (from everything else). It is known within the purified spirit soul by the sweet taste of Lord Caitanya's lotus feet.

Purport

The material mind has no power to realize how the Supreme can be both non-different and different from everything else. Why does it not have this power? The reason is that, in the material world, nobody comprehends mutually contradictory qualities residing in the same place. Thus, souls shackled to the material world, with knowledge of material things only, have no inclination to develop faith that mutually contradictory qualities actually reside in Bhagavān.

Such innumerable, mutually contradictory qualities, manifested by His inconceivable potencies, elegantly and joyfully exist in Bhagavān. He is the impersonal brahman without form, and He is a person also with a graceful and sublime form. He is tinier than the tiniest thing, and he is also bigger than the biggest thing. He is impartial but still loves his bhaktas. He is without qualities but also certainly has qualities. He is the impersonal brahmajyoti, and yet He is also Kṛṣṇa, the Supreme Personality, surrounded by many cowherd boyfriends. He is the supermost philosopher and complete with all knowledge, yet He is also a devoted lover, Whose whole transcendental being consists of love.

Bhagavān is the shelter where all of these qualities, as well as all of His other mutually contradictory qualities, reside. The Supreme is never to be compared to material entities. The conditioned soul imprisoned in the world of matter possesses an intelligence that consists of matter. Such intelligence has no power to contact that which is beyond the realm of matter. The conditioned souls shackled in this material world are thus unable to comprehend the qualities of Bhagavān. In this way, they have no faith that Bhagavān has a nature like this.

For the duration of their stay in the prison-house of this material realm, the individual, conditioned souls are unable to understand how Bhagavān is simultaneously and inconceivably one with and different from everything. Will conditioned souls, imprisoned by matter, never comprehend this point? The answer to this question is that those souls who taste the nectar of devotional service to the lotus feet of Lord Caitanya will eventually become purified, and, in this way, will gradually be able to understand it. In the process of becoming purified, the soul realizes his own original nature. At the time when he fully realizes it, he understands how Bhagavān is simultaneously one with and different from everything.

The phrase caitanya-caraṇāsvādāt appears to have two meanings, although, in point of fact, those two meanings are actually one. The first meaning is: "A person attains transcendental bliss by serving the lotus feet of Lord Caitanya." The second meaning is: "By serving the feet of the omniscient Supreme Personality of Godhead, a person attains transcendental bliss." The omniscient Supreme Personality of Godhead is non-different from Śrī Caitanya Mahāprabhu; therefore, these two meanings are actually one.

The opinions of different philosophers, all of whom are conditioned souls imprisoned within the material realm, were considered in the First Chapter of this book. Since I have now refuted all of their philosophies, I shall now describe the Supreme Absolute Truth, the spiritual Truth instructed by the Supreme Pure: Lord Caitanya Mahāprabhu.

cid eva paramaṁ tattvaṁ cid eva parameśvaraḥ /
cit-kaṇo jīva evāsau viśeṣaś cid-vicitratā //9//

The Supreme Absolute Truth and the Supreme Lord are spiritual. The spirit soul is a small particle of spirit in the great manifested variegatedness of the spiritual world.

Purport

The three divisions of eternal existence are spirit, matter, and the individual spirit souls. The Supreme Absolute Truth and the Supreme Lord are spiritual. The individual spirit soul is an infinitesimal part of spirit. In the spiritual world exists great variegatedness. Bhagavān is like a sun glowing in that spiritual world. The infinitesimal spirit souls are like the rays of light of that sun, like particles of that light; they are therefore all infinitesimal spirits. Great variegatedness is ever-present in the spiritual world, and nothing is superior to the spirit. Material variegatedness is only a perverted reflection of spiritual variegatedness.

ānandaś cid-guṇaḥ proktaḥ sa vai vṛtti-svarūpakaḥ /
yasyānuśīlanāj jīvaḥ parānanda-sthitiṁ labhet //10//

It is said that he (the soul) is blissful, full of spiritual qualities. Cultivating activities in accordance with his intrinsic nature, the liberated soul attains a position of topmost bliss.

Purport

Free will is one quality of spirit soul; bliss is another. That bliss is part of the intrinsic nature of spirit soul. Therefore, by repeatedly executing spiritual activities, an individual soul becomes blissful. In the Vedas it is stated: "When he understands the reservoir of all pleasure, he delights in that highest bliss."

The Vedas thus affirm that bliss is intrinsically part of the nature of spirit soul. Bliss is intrinsic to the nature of spirit soul just as burning power is intrinsic to the nature of fire and fluidity is intrinsic to the nature of water. Even conditioned souls shackled by matter enjoy a specific, material version of that bliss. Every entity has two features: One is its nature, and the other is its activities. Spiritual activities deliver spiritual bliss. The conditioned soul who repeatedly engages in blissful, spiritual activity eventually attains spiritual bliss. He becomes gradually eligible to enjoy the topmost bliss of personal association with the Supreme Lord, Bhagavān.

cid-vastu jaḍato bhinnaṁ svatantrecchātmākaṁ sadā /
praviṣṭam api māyāyāṁ sva-svarūpaṁ na tat tyajet //11//

The substance of spirit self always possesses independent desire (and) is different from inert matter. Even having entered the realm of illusion, that (self) still does not renounce his intrinsic nature.

Purport

How many times has the question been asked: What is the nature of spirit soul? A person in this material world is unable to discover the completely perfect answer. Despite the soul being spiritual, he has now forgotten his own intrinsic nature. Bound in the prison-house of Māyā, the conditioned soul finds it very difficult to present a clear answer concerning his own intrinsic nature. His nature is that of an infinitesimal part of the spirit whole.

The soul never actually renounces his own intrinsic nature, despite that nature being pervertedly reflected in the material realm. At the very beginning, this question may be asked: "Spirit soul must be different from material things, since he is different from matter—what is that difference?" A genuine seeker should first search out the answer to that question. There are many different qualities noticed in material things, but neither consciousness nor free will is ever seen in them.

Unless the conditioned soul is completely restricted in his activities, these two qualities remain uncovered and are manifest. A quality such as heat is seen in the material element of fire. Liquidity is seen in the material element of water. However, that liquidity is not the sign of free will present there; water is not liquid of its own accord. No material element, when all are considered, acts of its own free will.

However, considering the conditioned souls, who are ultimately spiritual beings, even though covered by material bodies in low species of life--such as that of worms or ants--we perceive that free will is present with them. Walking here and there, an ant considers in which direction he should go, and then he walks on that path. This power of the ant to think and choose are signs of free will, but we do not see such signs in dead matter.

We perceive them only in living beings, in spirit. Therefore, both consciousness and free will are part of the intrinsic nature of spirit soul; there can be no doubt about this. In conclusion, consciousness, free will, bliss, and the conception of "I am" are all parts of the intrinsic nature of spirit soul. Even when he enters the material realm of five gross elements, the conditioned soul cannot renounce that nature.

phalguṁ nirarthakaṁ viddhi sarvaṁ jaḍamayaṁ jagat /
bahirmukhasya jīvasya gṛham eva purātanam //12//

Please know that (this creation is) a prison-house since time immemorial. It has no reality and is of no genuine benefit to the conditioned soul, who is absorbed in the dead matter of this universal creation and has turned his face away from the Supreme.

Purport

The illusory material world is without any real meaning. It is a prison-house from time immemorial for the conditioned souls who have turned their faces from the Supreme. Śrī Vyāsadeva entered into a perfect trance, following Nārada Muni's instruction. In that trance, his heart purified by devotional service, Vyāsadeva saw the Absolute Truth, and this is described in ***Śrīmad-Bhāgavatam* (1.7.4-6):**

bhakti-yogena manasi samyak praṇihite 'male
apaśyat puruṣaṁ pūrṇaṁ māyāṁ ca tad-apāśrayām

"Without even a tinge of material inauspiciousness, by perfect engagement of his mind in devotional service, he (Vyāsadeva) saw the Supreme Absolute Person with His illusory energy (Māyā) under His complete control."

yayā sammohito jīva ātmānaṁ tri-guṇātmakam
paro 'pi manute 'narthaṁ tat-kṛtaṁ cābhipadyate

"By whom (Māyā) the living entity, in spite of being transcendental, is perfectly illusioned, taking for granted that his self is a product of the three material modes of nature. By them, he undergoes the reaction of experiences (material miseries) not at all wanted."

anarthopaśamaṁ sākṣād bhakti-yogam adhokṣaje

"The direct and complete cessation of these unwanted experiences (is attained) by engagement in devotional service to the Lord, Who is beyond the range of material perception."

The creation of Māyā, this material realm, is an illusory and useless place for the individual spirit souls, who are infinitesimal parts of spirit. Why do individual spirit souls make their residence in this useless place? The answer is that the material world is a prison-house from time immemorial for the individual souls who have turned their faces away from the Supreme; only they have entered this realm.

The liberated souls who do not turn away their faces from the Supreme Lord remain forever free from the material prison-house and do not enter it. They remain forever in the spiritual world. The potency of material illusion, the māyā-śakti, always remains under Lord Kṛṣṇa's control. As darkness must always remain far from the shining sun, similarly, the illusory potency of Māyā must remain forever far away from Lord Kṛṣṇa, a long distance from the spiritual world. Conditioned souls who have turned their faces away from the Supreme Lord Kṛṣṇa are attracted to, and bewildered by, the variegatedness of this world of Māyā.

That is the way in which they fall under the spell of Māyā. The individual souls are, in reality, always transcendental to the modes of material nature. However, when they fall under the spell of Māyā, they consider themselves products of the material modes. They then attempt to enjoy pathetic pleasures offered by those three modes. This is the condition of those conditioned souls who have turned their faces from the Supreme. The others, liberated souls, those who stay in the spiritual world, do not turn their faces from the Supreme. Only those souls who turn their faces from the Supreme Lord depart the spiritual world and enter the realm of inert matter.

deśa-kālādikaṁ sarvaṁ māyayā vikṛtaṁ sadā /
māyātītasya viśvasya sarvaṁ tac cit-svarūpakam //13//

Beginning with time and place, everything here is always undergoing perverted change by the illusory energy. Of that which is beyond Māyā, the whole of it is spiritual in nature.

Purport

The spiritual realm is far, far away from Māyā, but the material realm is the creation of Māyā. What is the relationship between these two realms? Our answer to this question is that time, place, and everything else in the material realm are all grotesque perversions. Far away from Māyā, however, time, place, and everything else in the spiritual world are all spiritual in nature. The meaning of this is that everything there is supremely pure.

There are many impediments to happiness in this grotesque material realm. As such, it is seen that the material world is extremely distorted and horrible. Here, time is divided into past, present, and future, and, according to that division, many entities are continuously destroyed; many kinds of suffering thus continuously emerge. In this way, the material realm is loaded with innumerable hideous and fearful manifestations; the whole show is horrible and ugly.

Time, place, and everything else is all-spiritual in the spiritual world; everything there is full of bliss, full of love. There is not even the slightest whiff of matter in the spiritual world. The spiritual world is elegantly described in the Eighth Chapter of the ***Chāndogya Upaniṣad*** as follows:

hariḥ om. atha yad idam asmin brahmapure daharaṁ puṇḍarīkaṁ veśma daharo 'sminn antarākāśas tasmin yad- antas tad anveṣṭavyaṁ tad vāva vijijñāsitavyam iti. taṁ ced brūyur yad idam asmin brahmapure daharaṁ puṇḍarīkaṁ veśma daharo 'sminn antarākāśaḥ kim tad atra vidyate yad anveṣṭavyaṁ yad vāva vijijñāsitavyam iti. brūyād yāvan vā ayam ākāśas tāvan eṣo 'ntar hṛdaya ākāśa ubhe asmin dyāv-āpṛthivī antar eva samāhite ubhāv agniś ca vāyuś ca sūrya-candra-samāv ubhau vidyun- nakṣatrāṇi yac cāsyehāsti yac ca nāsti sarvaṁ tad asmin samāhitam iti. taṁ ced brūyur asmiṁś ced idaṁ brahmapure sarvaṁ tad asmin samāhitaṁ sarvāṇi ca bhūtāni sarve ca kāmā yadaitaj jarāv āpnoti pradhvaṁsate vā kiṁ tato 'tiśiṣyata iti. sa brūyann asya jarayāitaj jīryati na vadhenasya hanyata etat satyaṁ brahma-puram asmin kāmāḥ samāhitā eṣa ātmāpahata-papma vijaro vimṛtyur viśoko vijighatso 'pipāsaḥ satya-kāmaḥ satya-saṅkalpo yathā hy eveha prajā anvāviśanti yathānuśāsanaṁ yaṁ yam antam abhikāmā bhavanti yaṁ janapadaṁ yaṁ kṣetra-bhāgaṁ taṁ tam evopajīvanti. tad yatheha karma-jito lokaḥ kṣīyate evam evāmutra puṇya- jito lokaḥ kṣīyate tad ya ihātmānam ananuvidya vrajanty etāṁś ca satyaṁ kāmāṁs teṣāṁ sarveṣu lokeṣv akāma-caro bhavaty atha ya ihātmānam anuvidya vrajanty etāṁś ca satyaṁ kāmāṁs teṣāṁ sarveṣu lokeṣu kāma-caro bhavati. sa yadi pitṛloka-kāmo bhavati saṅkalpād evāsya pitaraḥ samuttiṣṭhanti tena pitṛlokena sampanno mahīyate. sa yadi mātṛloka-kāmo bhavati saṅkalpād evāsya mātaraḥ samuttiṣṭhanti tena mātṛlokena sampanno mahīyate. sa yadi bhrātṛloka-kāmo bhavati saṅkalpād evāsya bhrātaraḥ samuttiṣṭhanti tena bhrātṛlokena sampanno mahīyate. sa yadi svasṛloka-kāmo bhavati saṅkalpād evāsya svasaraḥ samuttiṣṭhanti tena svasṛlokena sampanno mahīyate. sa yadi sakhiloka-kāmo bhavati saṅkalpād evāsya sakhāyaḥ samuttiṣṭhanti tena sakhilokena sampanno mahīyate. sa yadi gandhamālyaloka-kāmo bhavati saṅkalpād evāsya gandhamālye samuttiṣṭhanti tena gandhamālyalokena sampanno mahīyate. sa yady annapānaloka-kāmo bhavati saṅkalpād evāsyānnapāne samuttiṣṭhanti tena annapānalokena sampanno mahīyate. sa yadi gītavāditraloka-kāmo bhavati saṅkalpād evāsya gītavāditre samuttiṣṭhanti tena gītavāditralokena sampanno mahīyate. sa yadi strīloka-kāmo bhavati saṅkalpād evāsya striyaḥ samuttiṣṭhanti tena strīlokena sampanno mahīyate. yaṁ yam antam abhikāmo bhavati yam kāmayate so 'sya saṅkalpād eva samutiṣṭhati tena sampanno mahīyate. te ime satyāḥ kāmā anṛtapidhānās teṣāṁ satyānāṁ satām anṛtam apidhānaṁ yo yo hy asyetaḥ praiti na tam iha darśanāya labhate. atha ye cāsyeha jīvā ye ca pretā yac cānyad icchān na labhate sarvaṁ tad atra gatvā vindate 'tra hy asyaite satyaḥ kāma anrtapidhānas tad yathāpi hiraṇya-nidhiṁ nihitam akṣetrajña upary upari sañcaranto na vindeyur evam evemaḥ sarvāḥ prajñā ahar ahar gacchanty atra etaṁ brahmalokaṁ na vindanty anṛtena hi pratyudhaḥ. sa eva eṣa ātmā hṛdi tasyaitad eva niruktaṁ hṛdy ayam iti tasmād dhṛdayam ahar ahar vā evamvit svargaṁ lokam eti. atha ya eṣa samprasādo 'smāc charīrāt samutthāya paraṁ jyotir upasampadya svena rūpeṇābhiniṣpadyata eṣa ātmāti hovacaitad amṛtam abhayam etad brahmeti tasya ha vā etasya brahmaṇo nāma satyam iti. tāni ha vā etāni trīṇy akṣarāṇi satīyam iti tad yat sat tad amṛtam atha yad dhi tan martyam atha yady antenobhe yacchati yad anenobhe yacchati tasmād yam ahar ahar vā evamvit svargaṁ lokam eti. atha ya ātmā sa setur vidhṛtir eṣāṁ lokānām asambhedāya naityaṁ setum aho-rātre tarato na jarā na mṛtyur na śoko na sukṛtāṁ na duṣkṛtām. sarve papmāno 'to nivartante 'pahata-papma hy eṣa brahmalokas tasmād vā etaṁ setuṁ tīrtvāndhaḥ sann anandho bhavati viddhaḥ sann aviddho bhavaty upatāpī sann anupatāpī bhavati tasmād vā etaṁ setuṁ tīrtvāpi naktam ahar evābhiniṣpadyate sakṛd vibhato hy evaiṣa brahmalokaḥ.

cic-chakteḥ para-tattvasya svabhāvas tri-vidhaḥ smṛtaḥ /
sva-svabhāvas tathā jīva-svabhāvo māyikas tathā //14//

It is well known that there are three kinds of spiritual potency of the Supreme Absolute Truth: His own nature as well as the nature of the individual spirit souls as well as the nature of the illusory energy.

Purport

The nature of the Supreme Absolute Truth is threefold: His own nature, the nature of the individual spirit souls, and the nature of the illusory energy. There is variety without limit in the spiritual nature. The impersonalists known as Māyāvādīs do not consider that variety can be present in spirit. They proclaim: "Variegatedness is only present in Māyā. When a person gives up Māyā and turns to spirit, variegatedness is cast to a very great distance. All variegatedness disappears and everything becomes one when spirit attains its original nature."

On what foundation are these Māyāvādī concoctions based? What is the root from which they have grown? The answer is that these ideas are based only upon their whims. In what sacred scripture are these concoctions presented? By what chain of logical arguments can they be substantiated? That nobody can say.

In the lengthy Chāndogya Upaniṣad passage previously cited, we see a description of spiritual variegatedness. The form of the Supreme Personality of Godhead is present in the spiritual world, as well as the forms of individual spirit souls. There is a great variety of spiritual places there. There is the moon, sun, other luminaries, rivers, streams, and many other exalted and beautiful entities. Also found there are a great variety of spiritually blissful tastes.

The individual souls are the Supreme Lord's marginal potency; that is their constitutional position. They are situated between the spiritual and material potencies. As such, they may come under the influence of the Māyā potency or the influence of the spiritual potency.

Māyā is the perverted reflection of spirit; that is Māyā's nature. The individual spirit souls who have turned their faces away from the Supreme Absolute Truth, the Supreme Lord, are forcibly covered with gross and subtle material bodies.

tiṣṭhann api jaḍādhāre cit-svabhāva-parāyaṇaḥ /
vartate yo mahā-bhāgaḥ sva-svabhva-paro hi saḥ //15//

Even though situated here in the world of dead matter, a transcendentalist devoted to the spiritual nature is a greatly fortunate person. He indeed realizes his intrinsic spiritual nature.

Thus end the Bhaktivinode purports to the Second Chapter of ***Tattva-viveka***, entitled ***Realization of Eternal Consciousness.***

Appendix One

The Kumāras Meet Lord Padmanābha

In the Śrīmad-Bhāgavatam, there is a description of a spiritual region, one that is previous to the seventh gate of Vaikuṇṭha. This description is found in Chapters Fifteen and Sixteen of the Third Canto of that great work. Indeed, Chapter Fifteen is entitled, in his translation and commentary of this transcendental Purāna, "Description of the Kingdom of God" by His Divine Grace A. C. Bhaktivedānta Swāmī Prabhupāda.

All emphases added for your edification and realization.

In the thirteenth text of Chapter Fifteen, the following Sanskrit is found in the śloka itself: ***yayuḥ vaikuṇṭha-nilayam***. It is accurately translated to mean "***they entered the abode named Vaikuṇṭha***." The "they" being referred to here is the four Kumāras, and this previous pastime of his sons is being described (in both of these chapters) by their father, Lord Brahmā. Keep this Sanskrit and translation in mind as we continue on with this pastime.

The complete verse (3.15.13) was translated as follows:

"After thus traveling all over the universes, they also ***entered into the spiritual sky***, for they were freed from all material contamination. In the spiritual sky, there are spiritual planets ***known as Vaikuṇṭhas***, which are the residence of the Supreme Personality of Godhead and His pure devotees and are worshiped by the residents of all the material planets."

A little later in this chapter, in the purport to Text Fifteen, Prabhupāda comments:

"But ***in the Vaikuṇṭha world***, the spiritual sky, only the mode of goodness in its pure form exists. The Lord and His devotees reside ***in the Vaikuṇṭha planets***, and they are of the same transcendental quality, namely, śuddha-sattva, the mode of pure goodness. ***The Vaikuṇṭha planets*** are very dear to the Vaiṣṇavas, and for the progressive march of the Vaiṣṇavas toward the kingdom of God, the Lord Himself helps His devotees."

In his commentary to Text Nineteen, Prabhupada reiterates this transcendental theme:

"***In the Vaikuṇṭha world entered*** by the four Kumāras, even the birds and flowers are conscious of service to the Lord."

As such, it is perfectly clear that the Kumāras were already in Vaikuṇṭha from the very beginning of this description.

In text 26, Prabhupāda transliterates and translates the Sanskrit word ***tad*** to mean "Vaikuṇṭha." The complete translation reads:

"Thus the great sages, Sanaka, Sanātana, Sanandana and Sanat-kumāra, upon reaching ***the above-mentioned Vaikuṇṭha in the spiritual world*** by dint of their mystic yoga performance, perceived unprecedented happiness. They found that the spiritual sky was illuminated by highly decorated airplanes piloted by the best devotees ***of Vaikuṇṭha*** and was predominated by the Supreme Personality of Godhead."

This is further verification that the Kumāras had already entered the region of the spiritual world known as Vaikuṇṭha.

Then comes Text 27, where the plot thickens. The Kumāras, who are great sages, come to ***the seventh gate***. Please remember that they had been traveling through Vaikuṇṭha, the Vaikuṇṭha planets, a region described as having devotees, with spiritual forms, engaged in the glorification of the Supreme Lord.

"***After passing through*** the six entrances ***of Vaikuṇṭha-purī***, the Lord's residence, without feeling astonishment at all the decorations, they saw ***at the seventh gate*** two shining beings of the same age."

In a concise purport, Prabhupāda informs us:

"The sages were so eager to see the Lord within Vaikuṇṭha-purī that they did not care to see the transcendental decorations ***of the six gates which they passed by one after another***. But, at the seventh door, they found two doormen of the same age. The significance of the doormen's being of the same age is that, in the Vaikuṇṭha planets, there is no old age, so one cannot distinguish who is older than whom. The inhabitants of Vaikuṇṭha are decorated like the Supreme Personality of Godhead, Nārāyaṇa . . ."

In the following purport to Text 29, we find the four sages were not allowed to enter through the seventh gate:

"The childlike saintly personalities entered all the six doors of the palace, and no one checked them; therefore when they attempted to enter the seventh door and were forbidden by the doormen, who checked them with their sticks, they naturally became very angry and sorrowful."

In the purport to the next text, we receive further enlightenment regarding this awkward situation:

"Although they looked like five-year-old boys and traveled naked, the Kumāras were older than all other living creatures and had realized the truth of the self. Such saints were not to be forbidden ***to enter the kingdom of Vaikuṇṭha***, but, by chance, the doormen objected to their entrance. This was not fitting. The Lord is always anxious to serve sages like the Kumāras, but in spite of knowing this fact, the doormen, astonishingly and outrageously, prohibited them from entering."

We notice an apparent contradiction here. It has been established, beyond doubt, that these sages had already entered Vaikuṇṭha. However, now Prabhupāda says that they were being forbidden to enter the kingdom of Vaikuṇṭha. There can be no contradiction in the Absolute Truth. Indeed, it is the perfect resolution of this apparent contradiction that allows us to understand something very essential about our original position as jīva-tattva, the marginal potency or taṭasthā-śakti of the Supreme Lord.

In his commentary to Text 31, Prabhupada explains:

"In the previous verse, it has been clearly mentioned that the Kumāras were liberated persons. Viditātma-tattva means 'one who understands the truth of self-realization.' One who does not understand the truth of self-realization is called ignorant, but one who understands the self, the Superself, their interrelation, and activities in self-realization is called viditātma-tattva."

This stage and state of realization had also been described in the Bhāgavatam earlier, specifically in the Second Canto:

muktir hitvānyathā rūpaṁ sva-rūpeṇa vyavasthitiḥ

"Liberation is the permanent situation of the form of the living entity after he gives up the changeable gross and subtle material bodies."

In the text of śloka 34, the Kumāras conclude that the two doormen who were checking them from entering through the seventh gate should be dispatched to the material world:

"Since they find duality ***in the existence of Vaikuṇṭha life***, they are contaminated and should be removed from this place to the material world, where the living entities have three kinds of enemies."

The next verse reads:

"When the doormen ***of Vaikuṇṭhaloka***, who were certainly devotees of the Lord, found that they were going to be cursed by the brāhmaṇas, they at once became very much afraid and fell down at the feet of the brāhmaṇas in great anxiety . . ."

So, all of this transpired in Vaikuṇṭha, viz., the Kumāras traveling through the previous six gates, the transcendental regions that lay between those gates, and now, just outside the seventh gate, the astonishing pastime with the two gatekeepers there.

Text 37 informs us of the next major event:

"At that very moment, the Lord, who is called Padmanābha because of the lotus grown from His navel and who is the delight of the righteous, learned about the insult offered by His own servants to the saints. Accompanied by His spouse, the goddess of fortune, He went to the spot on those very feet sought for by recluses and great sages."

Now, let us proceed to Chapter Sixteen.

In Text Two of Chapter Sixteen, we get a hint that there is something special about the seventh gate of Vaikuṇṭha, even in relation to the gatekeepers of that door, who, technically, are standing outside of it. In his purport to this verse, His Divine Grace explains:

"Even when a living entity is ***promoted to Vaikuṇṭha***, there is still the chance that he may commit offenses. But the difference is that, when one ***is in a Vaikuṇṭha planet***, even if, by chance, one commits an offense, he is protected by the Lord. This is the remarkable fact in the dealings of the Lord and the servitor, as seen in the present incident concerning Jaya and Vijaya."

In other words, there is a clear indication here that these two personalities had been promoted to this position in Vaikuṇṭha, quite possibly from a previous sojourn in the material world. It is also stated that their being cursed as a result of some offense, in this case from the four child-like sages, was a remarkable development, particularly since they were now going to be sent (back again?) to the material world. Lord Padmanābha approves the decision of the Kumāras that his two gatekeepers must be sent down:

"These servants of Mine have transgressed against you, not knowing the mind of their master. I shall therefore deem it a favor done to Me if you order that, although reaping the fruit of their transgression, they may return to My presence soon, and the time of their ***exile from My abode*** may expire before long."

In his purport to this second verse, Prabhupada explains:

"From this statement, we can understand how anxious the Lord is to get his servitor ***back into Vaikuṇṭha***. This incident, therefore, proves that those who have ***once entered a Vaikuṇṭha planet*** can never fall down. The case of Jaya and Vijaya is not a falldown; it is just an accident. The Lord is always anxious to get such devotees ***back again to the Vaikuṇṭha planets*** as soon as possible."

Then we come to Text 32 of Chapter Sixteen, as well as the all-important purport so munificently given to us by Prabhupāda. In his stunning commentary, we receive an essential clarification, but the verse itself hints at it:

"After thus speaking ***at the door of Vaikuṇṭha***, the Lord returned to His abode, where there are many celestial airplanes and all-surpassing wealth and splendor."

Lord Padmanābha stayed at the door itself; he did not go outside of it in order to render His judgment. This door is obviously very important in terms of the transcendental layout of the spiritual world. Prabhupada adds, in the commentary:

"It is clear from this verse that all the incidents took place ***at the entrance of Vaikuṇṭhaloka***. In other words, the sages ***were <u>not</u> <u>actually</u> within Vaikuṇṭhaloka***, but were at the gate. It could be asked, 'How could they return to the material world if they entered Vaikuṇṭhaloka?' But ***factually they did not enter***, and therefore they returned. There are many similar incidents where great yogīs and brāhmaṇas, by dint of their yoga practice, have gone from this material world ***to Vaikuṇṭhaloka***—but they were not meant to stay there." Of course, Durvāsa Muni comes to mind here, after he offended Mahārāj Amburīśa.

However, let us stay with the Kumāras. They had not entered Vaikuṇṭha, but it was irrefutably stated previously, at the very beginning of the previous Chapter, that they had entered. Is this an irreconcilable contradiction? We think not.

Obviously, the spiritual territory previous to the abovementioned seventh gate, or up to and including the seventh gate itself, is still Vaikuṇṭha, ***but it is also a buffer region***. There are all kinds of devotees there. They are all engaged in glorifying the Supreme Lord, using their free will properly in order to do so. They are not merely insentient sparks of the brahmajyoti floating.

They are transcendentally engaged by their own choice in their transcendental forms, according to their transcendental natures. They are clearly liberated, and their activities are eternal, full of knowledge. Read the Fifteenth Chapter in its entirety if you doubt any of these assertions. These wonderful devotees are all experiencing transcendental bliss, but the bliss that the other devotees of the Lord, the ones beyond the seventh gate, are experiencing may very well be superior to the ānanda that these devotees, previous to the seventh gate, relish.

This account provides an authoritative and śāśtric solution to all the so many controversies swirling around origination. Why does the taṭasthā region of the jīva-tattva have to be the brahmajyoti?

Why does, as another speculative alternative opines, the buffer region have to be the virajā or Causal Ocean? We see clearly here that there is another, ***a higher buffer region***, as delineated in the topmost Purāna, the Śrīmad-Bhāgavatam. This region is called Vaikuṇṭha and yet it is also called a region previous to Vaikuṇṭha—or Vaikuṇṭha proper, if you will.

As such, we have translated the commentary of Srila Bhaktivinode, in Chapter Two, text five, as the buffer region. We are not the first translators to have done so, but, arguably, we are the first to have made an indepth explanation as to why.

Appendix Two

On Origination and Reason for the Fall

atra jīvasya tādṛśa-cid-rūpatva

"The jīva originally has a spiritual form like that of the Lord's."
His Divine Grace Śrīla Jīva Gosvāmī Prabhupāda
Śrī Tattva-sandarbha, Anuccheda 34

All emphases added for your edification and realization

cid eva paramaṁ tattvaṁ cid eva parameśvaraḥ /
cit-kaṇo jīva evāsau viśeṣaś cid-vicitratā //9//

"The Supreme Absolute Truth and the Supreme Lord are spiritual. The ***spirit soul*** is a small particle of spirit in the great manifested variegatedness ***of the spiritual world***."
His Divine Grace Śrīla Bhaktivinode Ṭhākur Prabhupāda
Tattva-viveka, Chapter Two, Text Nine

"Only those souls who turn their faces from the Supreme Lord ***depart the spiritual world*** and enter the realm of inert matter."
His Divine Grace Śrīla Bhaktivinode Ṭhākur Prabhupāda
Tattva-viveka, Chapter Two, Text Twelve, purport

"The jīva is pure, without material designations. He is not serving the Supreme Lord. He has no taste for serving the Lord, due to ***lack of knowledge.*** The propensity for serving the Supreme Lord is ***dormant***. The propensity for material enjoyment is not there, but ***indifference to the service*** of Hari and the seed of material enjoyment are present.

. . . the jiva revives remembering the lotus feet of Śri Kṛṣṇa . . . his lost Kṛṣṇa consciousness is revived . . . re-established as the servant of the Lord. . .

The jīva cannot remain indifferent forever by subduing devotional and non-devotional propensities. He therefore contemplates unconstitutional activities ***from his marginal position***. He is infected by impersonalism, but, due to neglecting the eternal service of the Lord--and thereby ***developing the quality of aversion*** to the Lord--he cannot remain fixed in that position. In this way, aversion to the Lord breaks his concentration of mind and establishes him as the master of this world of enjoyment.

Māyā, the external energy of the Supreme Lord, then induces the marginal living entity to enjoy this world through her covering and throwing potencies and thus shows the living entity the reality of being averse to the Lord's service."

His Divine Grace Śrīla Bhaktisiddhānta Sarasvatī Gosvāmī Prabhupāda: Excerpts from **Vaiṣṇava and Brāhmaṇa** in the Hari-jana-khāṇḍa

"He is ***fallen*** already ***from Vaikuntha planet***. He is fallen in this material world, and he is again trying to make progress." His Divine Grace A. C. Bhaktivedānta Swami Prabhupāda Lecture on **Śrīmad-Bhāgavatam**, 2.3.19 in Los Angeles, June 15, 1972

Devotee: ***In the spiritual sky***, when the living entity is in his pure state of consciousness . . . does something act upon him to make him illusioned at that point also?

Srila Prabhupada: Yes. Just like Jaya-Vijaya. They committed offense. . . So, we sometimes commit mistake. That is also misuse of independence, or ***we are prone to fall down*** because we are small.

His Divine Grace A. C. Bhaktivedānta Swami Prabhupāda Room conversation in Los Angeles on June 23, 1975

"Now, we wanted to enjoy this material world. We have fallen down, just like Jaya-Vijaya. Now we are trying to ***go back again***. Therefore we say, 'Go back to home, ***back to Godhead***.'"

His Divine Grace A. C. Bhaktivedānta Swami Prabhupāda
Lecture on **Śrīmad-Bhāgavatam** in Melbourne, May 22, 1975

"As fragmental parts and parcels of the Supreme Lord, the living entities also have fragmental portions of His qualities, of which ***independence*** is one. ***Every living entity . . . has . . . a minute form of independence***. By misuse of that independence, one becomes a conditioned soul, and, by proper use of independence, he is always liberated."

His Divine Grace A. C. Bhaktivedānta Swami Prabhupāda
Bhagavad-gītā As It Is, 15.7, purport

"There is a ***dormant attitude for forgetting Krishna*** and creating an atmosphere for enjoying independently. Just like at the edge of the beach: Sometimes the water covers, sometimes there is dry sand, coming and going. Our position is like that: Sometimes covered, sometimes free, just like at the edge of the tide."

His Divine Grace A. C. Bhaktivedānta Swami Prabhupāda
Addendum of letter to Madhudviṣa Swami, June, 1972

"Those who are in the brahman effulgence, they are also in the fallen condition. So, ***there is no question of falling down from a fallen condition***. When fall takes place, it means falling down ***from the non-fallen*** condition."

His Divine Grace A. C. Bhaktivedānta Swami Prabhupāda
Letter to Revatīnandan dāsa, June 13, 1970

"The words nijam padam are significant (Ed. Note: nijam—his own, padam—original position). The living entity, being part and parcel of the Supreme Personality of Godhead, has the ***birthright to a position in Vaikunthaloka or the spiritual world*** . . . After giving up one's body, one will ***return home***, back to Godhead. . . . As a spiritual person, such a devotee ***returns*** to the Personality of Godhead and ***plays and dances with Him***."

His Divine Grace A. C. Bhaktivedānta Swami Prabhupāda
Śrīmad-Bhāgavatam, 8.24.51, purport

Devotee: If Krishna did not want us to come, why are we here?
Śrīla Prabhupāda: ***Yes. You forced Krishna to allow you to come.***
His Divine Grace A. C. Bhaktivedānta Swami Prabhupāda Conversation after a **Bhagavad-gītā** lecture
June 27, 1974 in Melbourne, Australia

Śrīla Prabhupāda: Why we are in this material world? We are part and parcel of Krishna. We should remain with Krishna in the spiritual world. . .

Devotee: When we are in the spiritual sky and serving Krishna, ***we have a perfect relationship with Krishna***. What causes us to fall down in the material world . . .?

Śrīla Prabhupāda: Because you desire to fall down.

His Divine Grace A. C. Bhaktivedānta Swami Prabhupāda Conversation after a **Bhagavad-gītā** lecture in Melbourne, Australia June 25, 1974 in Melbourne, Australia

Except for the first four, all quotations courtesy
of Bhaktivedanta Book Trust folio

Appendix Three

On Modern Philosophies and Philosophers

In the treatise you have just read, Tattva-viveka, the author, Śrīla Bhaktivinode Ṭhākur, has pointed out the flaws or evils of some philosophies and philosophers opposed to the Absolute Truth, which is also known as Vedānta darśana. He has touched upon a wide range of atheistic, materialistic, and impersonal philosophies in his book. Some of those he emphasized; others, he barely mentioned.

With the exception of the Epicureanism of Cārvāka (or, perhaps, his hedonism), Śrīla Bhaktivinode has delved into more than merely a passing study of the philosophies and philosophers which were prominent in India at his time. As such, we now know much about the inherent flaws of Sāṅkhya, the apūrva of Jaimini, Vaiśeṣika, Nyāya, and the Yoga-śāstra written by Patañjali-ṛṣi.

Also covered were other Eastern or India-based doctrines, such as Buddhism, Jainism, the philosophy of Zarathustra, and Monist impersonalism. Nevertheless, these were not Western philosophies--although some Westerners promulgated a pessimistic philosophy that was quite similar to Buddhism.

This English edition of Tattva-viveka is meant for Western students interested in the highest occult and spiritual science. Therefore, we are more concerned with Western philosophers and the ideas pushed by them. Indeed, over and above the Eastern philosophers and philosophies just mentioned, the majority of the doctrines criticized by the Ṭhākur were indeed Western.

Here again, however, we should boil it down, in order to concentrate upon the essence. Western culture began in Greece, and practically no one disputes that. Ancient Egyptian culture was as much Eastern as it was Western—if not more so--but Greek culture adopted some particularly Western epistemologies, worship structures, values, and political experiments. Western culture has thus far gone through seven stages: The empires of the Greeks, Romans, and Byzantines, the Dark Ages, the Gothic epoch, the Enlightenment, followed by the Modern Age (of which we are now in its post-modern octave).

Tattva-viveka was written in 1893, and the Modern Age was only a little over fifty years old at that time (we calculate its initiation at the beginning of the fifth decade of the Nineteenth Century). As such, we should not be surprised that modern philosophers and their speculations would not be exclusively featured. Nevertheless, in terms of Tattva-viveka, this is the area of most interest, because it has had—and continues to have—the most influence upon us. We are thus more than a little obliged to know and understand its philosophical essence, in order to transcend such ignorant influences pushed by the host culture.

Śrīla Bhaktivinode mentioned Yangchoo and Sardanapolus, but these were Asian atheists from an ancient time. He also discussed Leucippus and his disciple Democritus, who were Greeks; Plato and Aristotle were similarly—and very briefly--mentioned in the same vein. Lucretius was a poet-philosopher of the Roman epoch. No thinker from either the Dark Ages or the Gothic Era was discussed in the text. All of the abovementioned personalities were from antiquity, and very few if any of their concepts now contribute to the bedrock of modern thought.

Many philosophers from the Age of Enlightenment, however, ***were*** discussed in Tattva-viveka. It makes perfect sense, as that age, although it had already passed by 1893, was still relatively recent. The effects of those philosophies would still have had at least some potency at the end of the Nineteenth Century.

Prominent Enlightenment thinkers such as Pierre Gassendi, Julian Offray de La Mettrie, Denis Diderot, Francis Holyoake, Thomas Paine, and George Buchner were mentioned by the Ṭhākur. Paul Heinrich Deitrich Von Holbach (Mirabond), unlike these others, was given some particular attention by Bhaktivinode. However, with this as the only exception, all of these philosophers were merely mentioned by name once, without further description. As men of the Enlightenment, they have exerted only very minimal influence on modern thought and culture.

Jeremy Bentham, the father of classic Utilitarianism, David Hume, the founder of Skepticism, and George Berkeley, the founder of Idealism, were also men of the Enlightenment, although the influence of Bentham slightly bled into modern thought. Still, Śrīla Bhaktivinode only mentioned Bentham in passing.

George Combe was a philosopher who straddled the Age of Reason and the Modern Age. His name was simply mentioned once, however, and he never became a prominent philosopher in the history of modern philosophy.

John Tyndall, Charles Bradlaugh (a committed atheist), Jacob Molescott, and the poet-philosopher Moritz Hartmann, were all active writers during the modern era. Again, the Ṭhākur simply mentioned each of them once, spending no font space analyzing their particular philosophical contributions.

Arthur Schopenhauer was a man who became philosophically prominent in later life, after the Modern Age had commenced. Nevertheless, as has been already pointed out, there is not that much difference between his philosophy and the teachings of atheistic Buddhism. Although somewhat popular in New Age circles, Buddhism is not at all integral to the culture of modern philosophy, especially in relation to its intrinsic secular progressivism.

Thomas Huxley was influential at the beginning of the modern era. His form of pre-determination in Materialism, although quoted in the book (to some extent), was also contemptuously dismissed by the Ṭhākur, given rather short shrift. It is a dubious proposition that Huxley's influence remains prominent in Western culture at this time. As such, we have made the decision not to give him any consideration here in Appendix Three, and we have made the same decision in relation to all of the abovementioned authors.

The two modern philosophers who, from our perspective, require special analysis would be Auguste Comte and John Stuart Mill. Indeed, we consider Mill to be the founder of the modern era, as his voluminous writings had been most influential in initiating many of the pillars of modern thinking. He is still oft-quoted in intellectual circles and publications in the West. Comte's influence has remained a bit more subtle, but it should also be noted that Śrīla Bhaktivinode Ṭhākur wrote more words attacking him in Tattva-Viveka than he did any other philosopher. There must have been reasons for that, and we are going to discuss those.

Auguste Comte (1798-1857) was a Frenchman who founded both Sociology and Positivism, each of which has become influential after the commencement of the Modern Era. Comte believed that there were laws of the mind, in terms of its evolution, that could objectively be discovered and then dovetailed for the betterment of mankind. Positivism was allegedly a philosophy of the heart over the head (indicating Sentimentalism), but its philosophical precepts do not at all lack intellectual themes.

He believed that man evolved through three stages: Theological (Monotheistic), metaphysical, and then Positivistic. He rejected a supernatural explanation of things as primitive thinking. In this supposed evolution, man moves from the state of the personal (theological or supernatural) to the state of the impersonal or abstract (metaphysical) and then to the state of culmination: Humanistic Positivism. As we all know, various forms of Humanism are strong value pillars within the modern mood.

The emphasis of Positivism is scientific, humanistic, and attention to details here on this plane; this differentiates it substantially from the prevailing ethos of the previous Age of Enlightenment. Competency to ascertain facts and amass scientific data, in order to further a love for mankind, is considered the progress of Sociology, which is emphasized in Positivism. Perfection of group relations is the ultimate goal. Nature is meant only to be improved, and a Supreme Lord has nothing to do with that. Here again, we see this strain of thinking as being very prominent in modernism.

Man is meant to become the arbiter of his own destiny in Positivism, within certain limits. A belief in Providence was an impediment, meant to be thrown out, as it invokes passivity and worship of a God who does not actually assist mankind in learning to love itself. Comte's motto was: "Love for the principle, order for the basis, progress for the end." Many modern people exude this very feeling. Certainly, the West's liberal, secular progressives have been heavily influenced by this kind of thought for well over a century.

Study of the cosmos is meant only for the betterment of humanity, and for no other reason, as man is the measure of all things (the essence of Humanism). Comte considered any study of the universal or the occult, particularly if it was meant for understanding a so-called God, to be irrational, retrograde, and highly immoral. He considered atheism to still be connected to the metaphysical stage, due to its inherent tendency of seeking final solutions to theological problems. Comte considered all such theological dilemmas to be nothing more than a waste of valuable time.

In this way, he was a humanistic Utilitarian—a quality that he had in common with Mill. Any speculation on the meaning of life, the "why," was considered non-progressive. Śrīla Bhaktivinode Ṭhākur pointed out that Comte was attempting to conduct a funeral rite of man's inherent curiosity about his situation in an immense and apparently unfriendly universe. Yet this very mentality of extinguishing metaphysical inquiry is actually quite common within Western intellectual circles today.

Mental improvement, according to Comte, was meant for human betterment on this plane, and all study and information must be verified through empirical evidence and experimentation. The laws of Sociology could be discovered, via the heart. Comte was a Sentimentalist, but he was, somewhat paradoxically, also an Empiricist. He believed that these laws must also be ascertained by assembling all of the facts connected to social thought. This is something that, once again, he had in common with Mill. Indeed, their approaches are surprisingly similar, especially since Mill—who sought to develop a perfect "science of society"—was profoundly influenced by Comte in this connection. The malefic, atheistic after-effects of these two men on the weltanschauung of the modern Western sociology have been profound.

At the time when Comte became influential, in the last two decades of his life, the seeds of Communism were just beginning to sprout. Comte actually liked Communism, because he believed that the common man, the worker, was the best Humanist, at least potentially. He felt that it was the worker who would effectively spread the doctrine of Positivism. The workers are men of the heart, not the head, and they are not so much absorbed in metaphysical thinking as are the intellectuals.

It was Enlightenment metaphysics that needed to be overcome at this time, and the worker could very well become the vanguard for this achievement. Dedicated workers would form provisional substitutes (in the form of clubs) for the Church, preparing the way for a new worship of mankind, rather than worship of some mythical "God." Indeed, in many respects, this is the very essence of Communism--and we all know how much influence Communism has had on Western thought for the last ninety years or more.

Comte believed that the only real knowledge was factual reality on this plane, knowledge of things in which we have objective experience. Ironically, one of the most virulent anti-Communist philosophers of this age, Ayn Rand, was influenced by Comte. She has had a profound influence on Western capitalistic culture in modern times. Her philosophy of Objectivism practically follows the precepts of Comte line for line. In this way, Comte's philosophy has worked its way into both of the opposed spectrums (Communism and Capitalism) within modern Western society.

As was brought out in Tattva-Viveka, Comte was a big believer in the worship of women, putting women on a pedestal above that of the male. Have we not seen this splashed throughout the propaganda of Western culture? The "spontaneous priestess of humanity," along with the workers subservient to them, would successfully usher in the triumph of Positivism. In the same vein, since worship and love of God tamps down worship of woman, it should best be given up. Of course, the common man does not want to give it up. Therefore, as pointed out by Bhaktivinode

Ṭhākur, Comte devised (like Jaimini) a temporary acknowledgement of a "God" that ultimately did not exist. Nevertheless, He should still be worshipped as if He actually did exist, for pragmatic reasons helpful to the ultimate triumph of Positivism.

It is this mentality--the essence of kaitava-dharma or cheating religion--that is arguably the most devastating aspect of Positivism. Yet, in the West, this idea and feeling is quite common. People profess belief in God and go to church (a smaller and smaller percentage, as each decade passes), but, in actuality, they don't believe in the Theism being espoused in those houses of worship. Instead, they engage there for pragmatic reasons, in order to keep the social and economic order going nicely. The ultimate purpose, of course, is kāma or sense gratification. Comte set the tone for this kind of worship in Positivism. All things considered, he has had a tremendous negative impact on the devolution of culture in the atheistic Modern Age of Western thinking.

"I will call no being good who is not what I mean when I apply that epithet to my fellow creatures, and, if such a being can sentence me to hell for not so calling him, to hell I will go."
John Stuart Mill

John Stuart Mill (1806-1873) was a progressive liberal firebrand during the Victorian Era in England. His name is most often associated with Utilitarianism, and, indeed, one of his many written works had that very title. Yet, the founder of Utilitarianism was not Mill, but Jeremy Bentham. Mill's father, James Mill, was a close friend of Bentham, who was both his mentor and sometime patron. John Stuart Mill bought into Bentham's Utilitarian concoction during his younger years, but he came to, in many ways, reject it after he reached early adulthood.

We consider Mill to be even more influential in the development of modern thought than was Comte. Indeed, we consider John Stuart Mill not as the founder of Utilitarianism, but of something much bigger: **The Founder of the Modern Era**. Like Comte, Mill favored the working man and tried, not very successfully, to help the working class while he was a member of Parliament (for the Liberal Party and for one term only). Mill promoted bills there that would have led to a more equal division of profits. He was the first man to advocate feminism in England (and ridiculed for it). However, as we can readily see, feminism has more or less triumphed at this stage of modernism everywhere in the Western world.

Mill favored a form of state capitalism, although unfettered capitalism did begin to rear its ugly head during his lifetime. He promoted cooperative agriculture and representative government. He was a flagrant abolitionist, as well. Mill was heavily involved, both philosophically and practically, as an economist, sociologist, and logician. His influence in these areas was pronounced even during his lifetime; that influence is still subtly present in these particular fields in the West.

His politics was considered radical back then, but that would not be considered the case anymore, particularly in post-modernism. Universal human suffrage (especially for women) was a major component of his advocacy. Mill espoused a working philosophy and lifestyle that was opposed to the influence of the clergy, and he favored birth control (he was jailed for distributing pamphlets about this subject). All of these have triumphed in the Modern Age.

Like Comte, Mill believed that nature must be improved upon, and this became a very common theme during the Nineteenth Century. Although he conceded that natural perfection was impossible, nature should nevertheless be constantly amended, manipulated, and improved by man's effort for the sake of his intentions and benevolence. This emphasis on overlording material nature through various plans (meant to progressively improve the amenities of man) was not prominent during the Age of Enlightenment; it is certainly prominent now, however.

Mill believed that the instincts or untutored feelings of man, similar to the tendency of nature and nature's creatures, had to be disciplined and overcome in order to achieve human excellence.

He opined that belief in the supernatural was of no assistance in this regard. As a hard-core Empiricist, he could discover no solid evidence of a God who controlled nature from behind the scenes, but he did not dismiss the idea in its entirety. Still, whether God existed or not, Nature had to be confronted and overcome through the sheer willpower of man in league with his developed intellect. This idea is certainly at the bedrock of the Modern Age.

Mill rejected scriptural evidence entirely, considering it to be a self-motivated production of men who used it to manipulate the gullible and dull-witted, those of less intelligence. He believed in scientific pursuit in order to ascertain cause and effect, and he was particularly keen to discover any and all laws governing the science of Sociology. However, Mill was not quite as hardcore as Comte: Mill believed that God may indeed exist, but, if so, He was not omnipotent.

In other words, Mill was under the influence, whether he was aware of it or not, of Zarathustra. He believed that God was not the cause of evil and was at war against it. To explain this more fully, Mill believed that God did not intend, and was not in control of, all that happens here. As such, man should best develop his own type of divine mentality, particularly in relation to the vicissitudes and obstacles posed by natural selection. He should fight and dominate Nature. Mill believed man could eventually overcome Nature in toto, and we are certainly, in the Modern Age, heavily impacted by the consequences of this erroneous mindset.

If God was infinite in His power, according to Mill, then there would be no evil in the world. Bhaktivinode Ṭhākur brought up this very subject in the text of this book. Thus Mill, who certainly was also a Humanist like Comte, theorized that the existence of evil, death, terror, and pain proved that God was limited in His power.

Mill was incapable of, and unable to come to, the realization—just as modern man is similarly inept—that the Supreme Lord does not actually create evil. It is man who actuates evil within and without himself. Then, in response, the Supreme Controller creates an evil situation as a reaction and penalty for man's rebellious attitude, ignorance, evil desires, and capricious actions. Modernism absolutely rejects this explanation, of course.

Although most men and women of today--especially in this post-modern epoch of hedonism, surrealism, avante-garde, and haute-coutre—utterly discard any possibility of a Supreme Controller, those who, at least outwardly, do profess belief in Him, consider Him, like Mill, to be involved in a creation that is not fully under His control. If God is actually everything, then everything would be good. As such, since everything is far from good, then God must be limited in His power.

The Theistic mindset is rooted in complete opposition to all of modern thought. What we think of as evil is actually ultimately good, ***because it is deserved***. We cannot see how it is ultimately good, however, due to lack of knowledge and a desire not to understand Reality. At no time can the Supreme Lord be subject to our judgment, but that is exactly what Mill was doing in his writings on this subject. The Supreme Absolute Truth is both Personal and All-Good Absolute. That axiom is considered to be part and parcel of a fanatical mindset by virtually all of modern man, but devoted sages and thinkers of today recognize clearly that modern man himself is heavily entangled in various forms of fanaticism.

Like Comte, Mill believed that theological thought was archaic, belief in the supernatural appropriate only for a previous stage of undeveloped humanity. He believed that this kind of faith was no longer required in order to make progress in life. Indeed, he went so far as to opine that right and wrong can be only ascertained by dropping any belief system rooted in the supernatural. He advocated that humans, when freed from these impositions, are automatically good in their motives and will do the right thing. This is also one of the pillars of modern-day ontology.

It is nescience.

Mill believed that conscience determines morality, along with the duty assigned by a culture of advanced human societies. His rationalization here was vague, despite utilitarian underpinnings. Fear of displeasing other men took precedence over fear of displeasing genuine theological authorities, and this is another important brick in the wall of Western thought.

Mill doubted the immortality of the soul; he said that there was no evidence for it and no evidence precluding it. As such, what we can experience and accomplish here is of utmost importance in and of itself. Humanism is rooted in this very misconception. The philosophy of experience and the rejection of intuition were at the heart of the teachings propounded by Mill. Those axioms are today the essence of Materialism, consumerism, atheism, agnosticism, Skepticism, Cynicism, and many scientific pronouncements.

Although, at the end of his life, he did not totally reject transcendentalism, he still pushed the idea that a religion of humanity would be superior, and have a much greater effect, than any of the supernatural or transcendental religions of previous ages. With man at the center—a free and cultured individual emanating unselfish feelings for his fellow man--a Golden Age of real religion could be ushered in. Although this mentality has today millions of acolytes throughout the West, we have not seen any of these predicted good results from it in the past two centuries.

One of Mill's most famous works was On Liberty, written in 1859. Mill advocated complete freedom for man, so that he could express himself as he pleased. In this freedom, he believed that natural competition amongst men would result in the triumph of the best ideas; survival of the fittest was endemic to his particular brand of Utilitarianism.

However, competition is not very conducive to freedom. No human being has complete freedom, but competition tends to stifle whatever he may have; competition is, by its intrinsic nature, an impediment and an obstacle to freedom of both expression and action. In illusion, our so-called freedom is fully dependent upon the māyā, but real freedom entails liberation from unnecessary laws otherwise imposed by material energy. Modern man does not know how to attain these kinds of real freedom, and, in no small part, this is due to the all-pervading influences of modern-day philosophers and their humanistic philosophies.

Mill believed in government by law and not by man, a modern concept. He was an advocate of republican institutions concerned for safeguarding representative government from the tyranny of special interests, plutocrats, and the mob rule of majority opinion. He was a radical progressive—not what we would call it now, of course—but a radical progressive for his time. His idea of progress was foreign to the Enlightenment, as its adherents were thinkers who considered all major events as being entirely predestined.

Mill's introduction (his own variety) of progressivism into the bloodstream of Western culture, in due course, affected and colored all of its philosophies, chief tenets, and processes even up to this day.

Mill became a humanist and a proponent of the logic of experience in no small measure due to the intellectual, cultural, and emotional influence of his wife. She died just before he published the abovementioned On Liberty, arguably his most famous treatise. He attributed her association for his evolved understanding of many previously proposed abstractions. Here we see his synchronicity with Comte, as well as the effects of mundane association of "liberated" woman on theosophical realization.

During the previous age, its leading thinkers declared that the fabric of human civilization would be better and stronger if reason replaced religion in it. Modernism rejects the certainty of the Enlightenment, however, and doubts the existence of an omnipotent Creator. It believes that everything in every sphere can be made new, and it is an age of mobilization, industrialization, secularization, and invention. The modern age rejects what it considers the Enlightenment's false rationality; it also questions the coherence, certainty, and harmony that the Enlightenment insisted upon in universal affairs.

Modern thinkers say that intellectuals of previous ages, especially during the Enlightenment, did not actually comprehend the complexity of the world and the universe—and particularly the place of man in it. Modern man is also antagonistic to any final authorities, especially the authority of a Supreme Controller and/or the pre-eminence of reason. Modernism advocates an intense and critical scrutiny of all such conceptions.

The philosophies of modern man are rejected in Tattva-viveka. These philosophies, as well as the philosophers who pushed them, were all influenced by, or completely steeped in, atheism. The purpose of life is missed by the atheist, and, just as importantly, he or she has to pay for all of his or her influence and misdeeds in the next life. That may not be a human life, either.

Mill believed that happiness could only be attained by developing virtues, and, wherever applicable, overcoming desires. He set the stage for many different modern variants of this principle. He believed that his brand of utilitarianism was only useful when enacted by practical reformers, representing conflicting political views, promoting competition of thought.

We are now in the post-modern phase of this modern era, but it should not be considered a different epoch. In post-modernism, traditional thought is entirely abandoned; existentialism, decadence, hedonism, and nihilism replace it more or less completely. Transcendence is the target of considerable criticism or neglect, especially those spiritual concepts crafted within the personal rubric. All philosophers and theologians who represent human responsibility to higher authority are suspect. Classical antecedents are rejected, even more than they were during the Age of Enlightenment. The modern age is a dangerous one for true occultists and devotees, and both Comte and Mill set the stage for much of this pandemonium.

This age is now characterized by mobilization, industrialization, secularization, fantastic communication devices, mind-boggling technology, all kinds of invention, continuous commerce, mundane knowledge, massive transportation facilities, and competitive business dealings of all varieties. All of that is seeped in Materialism and Atheism. Bhaktivinode Ṭhākur is warning us about this wrong path in his treatise, and he has taken to task various Western philosophers for having laid the groundwork of it. Auguste Comte and John Stuart Mill were the pre-eminent symbols of what is now a Western mindset in a post-modern world; we should consider the fact that these men have actually misled us by their speculations. Tattva-viveka does not mislead us, however, as it exposes a variety of philosophies opposed to the Absolute Truth of Vedānta darsāna, providing us powerful hints as to how we can personally correct our course to real and eternal advantage.

"They're not changing their consciousness. They're not changing themselves inside. They're just changing their 'ism' from Communism to Capitalism and from Capitalism back to something else 'ism.' We're asking people to try to get a little bit beyond that superficial political system and find out what actually motivates each and every one of us. That is God consciousness, or love of God. That love of God is much more powerful than any temporary political system."

His Divine Grace A. C. Bhaktivedānta Swami Prabhupāda
Lecture at La Trobe University on July 1, 1974

Appendix Four

Srila Bhaktivinode Thakur: His Life and Precepts

Oṁ Viṣṇupāda Paramahaṁsa Śrīla Sac-cid-ānanda Bhaktivinode Ṭhākur Prabhupāda, the author of Tattva-viveka, made his transcendental appearance in this material world on September 2, 1838, a Sunday, in the village of Birnagar, also called Ulāgrām or Ulā, in the Nadia district of West Bengal, India. Birnagar is close to the blessed city of Navadvīpa. Bhaktivinode was the third son of Ānanda-candra Dutta and his wife Jagat-mohinī.

Although born in an illustrious, well-educated, and wealthy family, he suffered some miseries and ordeals throughout youth. At birth, he was given the name of Kedaranāth, which is another name for His Lordship Śiva, the Supreme Personality of Servitor Godhead.

Bhaktivinode was a nitya-siddha eternal associate of the Supreme Savior of Humanity for this Age of Kali, Lord Śacīnandana Śrī Caitanya Mahāprabhu. In order to rescue the true view from all the confusion so prevalent in his day, Śrīla Bhaktivinode rejuvenated the bona fide Kṛṣṇa consciousness movement begun by Lord Caitanya four hundred years earlier in India. In fact, he was directly sent by Lord Caitanya from the spiritual world for this very mission. Śrīla Bhaktivinode Ṭhākur was the first Ācārya to urge his fellow Vaiṣṇavas to preach the message of Kṛṣṇa consciousness in the West. He was also the first great devotee to translate Vaiṣṇava literature and poetry into the English language.

Tattva-viveka was written when the Ṭhākur was fifty-five years old, one of over one hundred forty books, manuscripts, commentaries, or poems penned by this extraordinary writer and śaktyāveśa-avatār. By his transcendental activities, words, and especially through his writings, this prominent Ācārya set in motion once again the flow of the bhakti-bhāgīrathī. In the modern age (now in its post-modern stage), perfectly representing the Six Gosvāmīs of Vṛndāvan, the Ṭhākur has kept the current of pure devotion going and is known as the Seventh Gosvāmī.

Since the time of the incarnation of the Supreme Personality of Godhead, Lord Caitanya, the great spiritual masters or Great Ācāryas in His line of disciplic succession have been, in chronological order, Rūpa Gosvāmī, Raghunātha dās Gosvāmī, Kṛṣṇadāsa Kavirāj Gosvāmī, Narottama dās Ṭhākur, Viśvanātha Cakravartī Ṭhākur, Jagannātha dās bābājī, Bhaktivinode Ṭhākur, Gaura Kiśora dās bābājī, Bhaktisiddhānta Sarasvatī Gosvāmī, and, most recently, His Divine Grace A.C. Bhaktivedānta Swami Prabhupāda. As we can see from this list, Bhaktivinode Ṭhākur was the seventh in the succession.

In his autobiography, he summed up his early childhood as follows: "My maternal grandfather had incomparable wealth and a grand estate. There were hundreds of male and female servants. When I was born, I was a good weight. I had an older brother, Abhayakali, who had previously died, and a second brother, Kaliprasanna, was still living. I was my father's third son.

It was said that, of all my brothers, I was a little ugly. But my mother said, 'Very well, let this boy be the servant of the rest. Just let him live a long time.' My mother told me that, when I was eight months old, I got a boil on my thigh, and, as a result, I became weak and emaciated. I also heard that while I was being carried in the arms of my nurse, Śibu, down a flight of stairs, I cut my tongue on my teeth. To this day I have a scar. This happened around the time my teeth were coming in."

Bhaktivinode Ṭhākur, while still known as Kedarnāth Dutta, became an expert linguist, fully conversant in English, Hindi, Urdu, Oriya, Bengali, Sanskrit, and even the Persian language. He had a proclivity for historical research in its application to the Absolute Truth. He assimilated the Purāṇas, as well as the speculative writings of ancient thinkers and modern European authors. He developed a knack for uncovering every facet of whatever subject matter actuated his transcendental interest, and he was meticulously thorough in all of his endeavors connected to any of this important research.

He became particularly active in his early adulthood at a critical time for Vaiṣṇavism in India. It was a negative historical juncture where the true teachings of Lord Caitanya had been almost completely covered, by time, in the form of three powerful forces. One of these was the British occupation, powerfully anti-Vedic in general and anti-Vaiṣṇava in particular. Another was the warped practices and behaviors of the pseudo-Vaiṣṇava sahajiyās of that day, who had become prominent after the disappearance of Visvanātha Cakravartī Ṭhākur.

The third and most powerful covering was a general abhorrence of Vaiṣṇavism by the people at large, due to both of the previously mentioned factors combined with their own inclinations to enjoy material life. The host culture had rejected Lord Caitanya, the sahajiyās had warped it beyond recognition, and British chauvinism was stamping its own forms of sophisticated culture onto the people.

The teachings of Lord Caitanya were being barely preserved by a handful of bābājīs, who were themselves very reclusive. In fact, the Ṭhākur was unable to procure a copy of Śrī Caitanya-caritāmṛta in manuscript form for many years. However, Bhaktivinode rejuvenated these teachings, and he re-discovered the birth-site of Lord Caitanya in the process. He then once again widely disseminated the pure and perfect knowledge. He even managed to get one of his books into North America, no small feat.

The Ṭhākur decided to enter into civil service under the patronage of the British ruling elite, a controversial--but, nevertheless, effective--move. Although he was an intellectual and scholarly philosopher at heart, he became a responsible Deputy Magistrate of the then occupational Government. As a magistrate, he was transferred from place to place in the government's service.

From such a position of a respected avocation and its accompanying financial strength, Kedarnāth Dutta was able to gradually infiltrate Kṛṣṇa consciousness into society at large through various writings and organizational activities. He published the first edition of his Vaiṣṇava journal, the Sajjana-toṣaṇī, in 1884. The next year, he founded the Vaiṣṇava Sabhā in Calcutta, his devotional society.

All this time, he was also married and had been raising children, eventually numbering twelve. With his publication of the authentic works of the Six Gosvāmīs of Vṛndavān, with his aforementioned discovery of Lord Caitanya's birthplace, with his effective door-to-door preaching campaign throughout the villages of Bengal, and with the successful spiritual education of his prominent son, Bimal Prasād Dutta (later known as Śrīla Bhaktisiddhānta Sarasvatī Gosvāmī), Kedarnātha Dutta became known, throughout Vaiṣṇava society and history, as Śrīla Bhaktivinode Ṭhākur.

He both predicted and desired that Westerners would one day come to Māyāpur in order to chant the Holy Name and take advantage of unique opportunities for spiritual advancement at the birth-site of the Supreme Personality of Godhead, Lord Caitanya. This prediction came to pass in the second half of the Twentieth Century.

He did the needful, applying a unique kind of devotional method in his preaching. For some time, he even associated with impersonalists for his own purposes. Whatever he did was spiritually perfect according to time, place, and circumstance, and there was never any contradiction in his activities.

He said that man's glory was in his common sense. He also said that everyone can engage in family or even worldly life, but he has to abandon destructive habits while doing so. Śrīla Bhaktivinode Thākur also insisted that advancement of material knowledge is a catastrophe, rendering a person more foolish than he was before. It causes him to forget his real identity, to become more entangled in material existence without any hope for liberation.

He said that material opulence is the expansion of Māyā's influence, and that every devotee, whether householder or sannyāsī, has to renounce such opulence. Indeed, the Thākur insisted that, in this age of Kali, it is preferable to be a householder in order to make progress in spiritual life. Although he was a householder with a large family, his Kṛṣṇa consciousness was notably superior to any of the sannyāsīs of his time. All the statements of Thākur Bhaktivinode are as good as Vaiṣṇava scriptures, because he was a liberated personality.

In Orissa, Ṭhākur Bhaktivinode also punished a self-proclaimed incarnation of Viṣṇu, who was imitating rāsa-līlā, engaging in sexual exploits with young girls. This powerful yogī was also seducing some less intelligent people into accepting him as the Supreme Lord. The yogī had developed a bit of a mystic power and was able to breathe fire from his mouth.

As magistrate, Bhaktivinode called the yogī to appear before him. "You say you are Lord Viṣṇu? If you are, then why don't you go live with Lord Jagannāth at the temple?" The yogī replied that he had no interest in idols.

Bhaktivinode thus knew that the man was an imposter, and he had him imprisoned for deviant behavior and fraud. Bhaktivinode's family members then became seriously ill, and this seemed to be the result of a curse from the yogī. The illnesses continued for a couple of days, and foolish people began to fear that maybe the fire-breathing yogī was actually Viṣṇu--and the Thākur had committed a great offense. Bhaktivinode did not flinch, assuring his family that all soon would be well. The powerful yogī then confessed that he was indeed an imposter, and Bhaktivinode punished him severely.

It was the desire of Bhaktivinode Thākur that the Caitanya movement be propagated all over the world. In 1875, he predicted that someone would come very soon who would individually preach it in this way. That prediction was fulfilled by Srila A. C. Bhaktivedānta Swami.

Bhaktivinode Thākur eventually was appointed magistrate of the city of Jagannātha Purī and superintendent of the Jagannātha temple. He thus had a very busy daily schedule. He slept short and wrote his books at night. He penned a small book called Śrī Caitanya Mahāprabhu and wanted to distribute it to Western universities. He was finally able to do so at McGill University in

Canada in 1896, the very year that Bhaktivedānta Swami took birth.

He empowered his son, Śrīla Bhaktisiddhānta Sarasvatī Gosvāmī Prabhupāda, in pure Kṛṣṇa consciousness, and he, in turn, empowered Śrīla Prabhupāda to preach in the West. As such, we can also consider that Bhaktivinode Thākur empowered Śrīla Prabhupāda and thus enabled all of us to come into contact with the Absolute Truth.

Śrīla Bhaktivinode Ṭhākur never formally took the order of sannyāsa. He eventually became a bābājī, living in seclusion away from wife and family as paramahaṁsa-ṭhākur. He did not complete the commentary of his last literary work and abruptly shut himself up in his beach-front cottage at Jagannātha Purī. He left this material world in 1914. There is a samādhi memorial erected in honor of the Ṭhākur at his house near the Jalāṇgi River.

A Calcutta High Court Judge of the name Śārada Charan Mitra was a friend of the Ṭhākur. He supplied Bhaktivinode with valuable Vaiṣṇava manuscripts. In his 1916 Introduction to a biography of Bhaktivinode Ṭhākur, entitled <u>A Glimpse into the Life of Ṭhākur Bhakti Vinode</u>, Mr. Mitra wrote: "I knew Ṭhākur Bhaktivinode intimately as a friend and a relation. Even under pressure of official work as a Magistrate in charge of a heavy subdivision, he could find time for devotional contemplation and work, and, whenever I met him, our talk would turn in a few moments to the subject of Bhakti and Dwaitādwaita-vāda and the saintly work that they lay before him. Service of God is the only thing he longed for and service under Government, however honorable, was to him a clog."

All quotations courtesy of Bhaktivedanta Book Trust folio

OM TAT SAT

10075999R00068

Made in the USA
Lexington, KY
18 September 2018